小经典译丛

U0693255

（汉英对照版）

青　春

［英］约瑟夫·康拉德　著　　梁遇春　译

辽宁人民出版社

Youth

by Joseph Conrad
Translated by Liang Yuchun

Ⓛ Liaoning People's Publishing House

图书在版编目（CIP）数据

青春 /（英）约瑟夫·康拉德著；梁遇春译. —沈阳：辽宁
人民出版社，2017.1（2020.6重印）
（小经典译丛）
ISBN 978-7-205-08787-6

Ⅰ.①青… Ⅱ.①约… ②梁… Ⅲ.①短篇小说—英国—近代
Ⅳ.①I561.44

中国版本图书馆CIP数据核字（2016）第276275号

出版发行 **辽宁人民出版社**
地址：沈阳市和平区十一纬路25号　邮编：110003
电话：024-23284321（邮　购）　024-23284324（发行部）
传真：024-23284191（发行部）　024-23284304（办公室）
http://www.lnpph.com.cn
印　刷：山东华立印务有限公司
幅面尺寸：110mm×180mm
印　张：5.125
字　数：68千字
出版时间：2017年1月第1版
印刷时间：2020年6月第2次印刷
责任编辑：刘国阳
封面设计：展　志
版式设计：姿　兰
责任校对：吴艳杰等
书　号：ISBN 978-7-205-08787-6
定　价：18.00元

出版说明

　　纵观中外翻译史，翻译活动与语言的发展密不可分。英语发展的各个重要阶段，翻译都发挥了重要作用，不仅丰富了英语的词汇，又极大地增强了英语的表现力。反观我国，古代的佛经翻译对汉语的用词、句法等均产生了影响。胡适的《白话文学史》中讲到，"维祇难，竺法护，鸠摩罗什诸位大师用朴实平易的白话文体来翻译佛经，但求晓易，不加藻饰，遂造成一种文学新体"。我国19世纪中叶起有意识地译介西方的地理、历史、政治、法律、教育的书籍，这些翻译活动大大丰富了汉语中的词汇，很多词汇已经融入日常用语并沿用至今，如"文学""法律""政治""铁路""贸易"等。到了19世纪末期和20世纪初期，梁启超所倡导的"新文体"对当时的读书人有着相当大的影响，而所谓"新文体"即是融合了浅近文言、翻译输入新名词、叙述自由、不合"古文义法"的文体。"小经典译丛·民国名家名译"所精选的翻译作品，就是在这样的背景下诞生的。无论是徐志摩还是郁达夫，均是从小耳濡目染着"新文体"同时又接受了良好的文言和外文的教育。因而，他们的译文既融合了本人母语写作的诗化、含蓄、连绵的特点，也将欧化的语言带入译文。从他们的译文中足以管窥汉语白话文推演之一斑。20世纪30年代语言学家钱玄同谈及汉语过渡时期，曾说应"用某一外国文字为国文之补助"；论及所选语种，则谈"照现在中国学校情形而论，似乎英文已成习惯，则用英文可也"。故而当时的一些知识分子也在译介域外文学时自觉地通过翻译来"改造"语言，例如周作人所倡导的"直译"等。无论是顺应西文词序不自觉地翻译，还是对汉语白话有意识地"改造"，都使这一时期的作品彰显了独特的语言气质——自由、含蓄、唯美、诗意，虽然不能妄言达到"信、达、雅"之境，却也力求用最精到的用词和与原文灵魂契合的句式，用独具风韵的白话进行表达。这也在某种程度上为这些名家的母语创作提供了借鉴。从徐志摩和郁达夫等人的现代诗和散文作品中，也能见到这种语言"改造"的影子。

　　尽管在习惯了现代汉语行文的读者看来，这些名家的译文多有机巧、不够平易，甚至有些不通，但如果放在当时的背景之下，就可以客观评价和欣赏这种文风的妙处。另外，民国初期很多地名、人名等尚没有严格的规范译名，尤其在文学翻译里，常见到译者别具匠心的音译或直译，虽缺少了规范，略有理解障碍，但这种自由也促成了一些精妙的译名诞生，如"翡冷翠"（佛罗伦萨）、"沁芳"（交响乐）这样的灵动传神，恐在今天一定是不合规矩、不合时宜的了。

　　丛书甄选这一时期名家的译介作品，编排名篇的中英文对照，旨在为喜爱欣赏文学和英文的读者提供中英文对照的素材，从比照原文和译文

了解名家甄选原文、推敲译文的良苦用心，近距
离感受他们的文化底蕴，并从中体会 19 世纪末
20 世纪初世界新旧交替、风云激荡的大背景下，
中国文人与学者的趣味和心境。浏览这套丛书，
不仅可以品读双语文学经典，还可借此回溯现代
文化一路发展的长河，于浪涛中取这一杯啜饮。

　　丛书编辑过程中，尽量保留了译著的原状，
借此为读者呈现民国初期珍贵的语言面貌。编辑
过程中仅对个别生僻词句加注说明，并对译文的
形式略有改动，如删去了《古代的人》原译中的
部分英文括注，以避免与原文对照功能重复。

　　不足与疏漏之处，敬请读者批评指正。

辽宁人民出版社

代　序

　　几个月前，受辽宁人民出版社编辑邀约，为他们精编的一套民国名家经典译丛作序，并收到电子初稿小样。虽执教英文近30年，翻译专业书籍、英美小说、杂文等文字量近200万字，但为学贯中西的大文学家、民国时期精英才俊郁达夫、徐志摩、林徽因等人的译作写序，岂敢？故几番推辞，不敢承约。但手中拥有了这份来自故乡的电子书小样，我如获至宝。在北欧夏日极昼极长的日光里，工作之余，悠闲地坐在斑驳树荫下、湖边草坪上或街边咖啡座里，我先睹为快。捧书细读，重温英汉对译的妙与美，我似乎穿越到了上个世纪二三十年代的民国时期，与我少年时起就崇拜的冷峻的郁达夫、才情的徐志摩和美丽的林徽因在方方正正的中文里相遇啦！我在字里行间感受民国时期那股清新的译风，在诗化的素美语言中玩味彼时翻译的乐趣，徜徉在看似信手拈来却也处处机巧的篇章中，时空仿佛凝滞在那精读时刻。

年少时，也曾读过英文原著小章节。一路走来，人生中年，在英语语境中深入到久远的原著，伴着波罗的海海边的余晖，我再一次理解郁达夫作品《沉沦》与他的译作《幸福的摆》的某种关联。主人公华伦徘徊在理性与感性之间，命运从悲喜转为平和，仿佛那身边大海，时而惊涛拍岸，汹涌澎湃，而后又归于平静安详，不禁抒发感叹：这就是人生啊！

某个晴朗的周末，我在湖边草坪席地而坐，像个12岁的小姑娘般充满好奇地读完了亨德里克·威廉·房龙撰写、林徽因译就的《古代的人》。房龙像个博学的圣诞老人，精巧细致地引领读者走入历史长河，贴切的行文勾画人类进步的面面观。而时年22岁的美丽才女林徽因用她缜密的逻辑、精致的文字、纯熟的译法再现原著风格。读她的作品如同欣赏她设计的精美建筑，那样灵动，那样飘逸。

徐志摩的诗才尽人皆知，他的字句清新、意境优美和神思飘逸，历来是文青们效仿的典范。美慧的英国女作家曼殊斐尔人格的精华给了诗人灵澈，他们惺惺相惜。最适合在一个绵绵细雨的日子，捧一杯咖啡或清茶，读《园会》，品《一杯茶》，看《理想的家庭》之模样。诗人用他如诗般的音律，典雅的人名转译，神奇点睛之笔，重现多位栩栩如生的欧美人物形象，亲切而又陌生，仿佛老上海城隍庙游园会，走来一群曼妙的蔷媚，谈着雨夜的翡冷翠……

　　快生活时代，让我们的思想、思绪慢下来，品读经典，体会文字语言的译介之美。让这译介的"媒"引领我们走入东西方文化的"国际理解"之中吧！

张东辉

（英语教授、维尔纽斯大学

孔子学院中方院长）

于维尔纽斯

2016年7月

目　录

青 春

这件事只能发生于英国，别的地方都不行，因为在英国，人同海可以说是互相贯穿——海走进许多人的生活里面去，人们也都知道一些，也许完全晓得，海上的娱乐，海上的旅行，或者海上挣面包的生涯。

我们围着一个乌木桌子，它反映出酒瓶，红葡萄酒酒杯，同我们的脸孔，当我们倚肘而坐。一个是公司经理，一个是会计员，一个是律师，一个叫做马罗，还有一个是我。公司经理从前是昆威船上的水手，会计员在海上服务过四年，律师——一个值得敬爱的根深蒂固的保守党，高派教会信徒，是一个极好的老头子，一位知耻的君子——曾经当俾·奥公司船上的大副，在从前好日子时候，那时邮船最少有两只桅装了横帆，常乘一阵合式的时令风走下中国海，低处高处都安有许多补助帆。我们大家起始都是靠着商船谋

生。所以在我们五个人里面，有海这个坚固的
关系，还有同行的友谊，这种亲切之感是对于游
艇、航行取乐和其他海上玩意儿的任何热心都不
能给的，因为一个只是人生的游戏，而那个却是
人生本身的事情。

马罗（最少我相信他自己是这样拼他的名
字）说出某一次航行的故事，或者还是说某一次
航行史比较妥当些：

"是的，我也见过一些东半球的海；但是我
记得最清楚的是我第一次到那里去的航行。你们
诸位知道有些航行好像是上天安排好来做人生的
解释，它简直可以说是人生的象征。你奋斗，你
工作，你出汗，你几乎把自己杀死，有时的确把
你自己杀死，只是为着要干一件事情——而结果
你不能成功。并不是因为你有什么错处。你无非
什么也做不好，无论大小的事情——简直世界上
没有一件事你能够做——甚至于连娶一个老处
女，或者把无聊的六百吨煤运到原定地的港口都
办不到。

"那次航行从头到尾是个值得纪念的事情。
那是我第一次到东方去的旅行，又是我第一次当

二副的航行；又是我船主第一次带船。你们会承认这是个极有意思的时候。他最少也有六十岁了；一个身材矮小的人，背宽大，却不很直，肩膀弯着，一只腿比那只腿更往外曲，他有那种绞扭的形态，在田地上工作的人们所常具有的。他有一副像破坚果的家伙的脸孔——下巴同鼻子想相遇，把陷进去的嘴遮住——脸的四围有绒毛一样的铁灰色须发，那好像洒有煤灰的棉织围巾。他这副古老脸孔里有一双蓝色的眼睛，出奇的活像一个小孩的眼睛，具有一种坦白的神情；有些很普通的人们靠着天生难得的纯洁心地同正直胸怀能够一直到死都保存着这种情调。什么使他肯雇我当船员，的确是件奇怪的事。我刚从一条走奥斯大利亚洲的上等快帆船出来，我在那里当三副，他对于上等快帆船好像有个偏见，认为是贵族的，时髦的。他对我说：'你知道，在这条船里，你得工作。'我说我一向无论到哪一条船都得工作。'啊，可是这里的工作跟你所说的不同，而且你们这班从大船出来的先生们……好罢！我敢说你干得下。明天来加入罢。'

"我第二天去加入。这是二十二年前的事情；

那时我才二十岁。时间过得多么快呀！那是我一
生里最快乐日子里的一个。请想一想！第一次当
二副——一个真真有责任的职务！我不肯把我这
个新任命状拿去换百万家产。大副仔细地把我打
量一下。他也是个老头子，但是另外一个派头。
他有罗马人的高鼻子，雪白的长胡子，他的名字
是马洪，但是他坚持这个字该念做冒纳。他的亲
友很有权势；然而他的命运总不好，他老没有
成功。

"至于船主，他有许多年头都在海岸上来往
的小船里，后来到地中海去，最后走进西印度群
岛的商船。他从来没有绕过好望角。他只能写出
麻糊的字，根本就不大注意写字。这两位当然都
是极好的海员，夹在这两个老汉之中，我觉得像
一个小孩子跟两个当祖父的人们一起。

"船也是古老的。它的名字是犹太。这是一
个奇怪的名字吗？它属于一个叫做维尔麦的人，
也许是叫做维尔可克斯——大概总是这类的名字
罢；但是他破产了，死了，已经有二十年了，或
者还要多些，他的名字也是无关紧要的。这只船
起先在沙德卫尔小池塘里搁了不少时候。你们可

以想象出它的情形。它满身都是铁锈，尘埃，垢腻——上面有烟泥，船面有污秽东西。对于我，这好像从一座皇宫出来，走进一所颓废的茅屋。它是四百吨左右的船，有一个简陋的绞盘车，门闩都是木做的，整个船没有一点洞，有一个四方形的大船尾。船尾上用大字写出它的名字，下面有许多云形装饰，泥金已经脱落了，还画有某种徽章，底下有一句铭语：'工作，否则灭亡。'我记得我非常喜欢这句话。这里面含有浪漫的情绪，有一种色彩使我爱这个老东西——有一种色彩感动了我少年的心境。

"我们离开伦敦时船上带个镇船重物——沙包——去北方一个海港装上煤运到盘谷（曼谷——编辑注）去。盘谷！我高兴极了。我在海上已经有六年了，但是只见到墨尔本同悉德尼，很好的地方，也各有它的妙处——但是怎么能比得上盘谷呢！

"我们扬帆乘着顺风驶出泰晤士河，有一个北海的引港者在我们船上。他的名字是泽明，他整天躲在船上厨房里面，借着炉火烘干他的手巾。他分明没有睡觉。他是一个悲愁的人，总有一粒眼泪挂在他鼻子尖端发光着，他也许曾经遇到灾难，或者正在灾难之中；或者预料将有灾难来临——不会高兴，除非有什么乱子出来。他瞧不起我的年青，我的常识，同我的驶船本领，一定要用几十个态度来表示他的不信任。我敢说他的意见是对的。我现在觉得那时我知道得很少，现在也没有多知道了许多；但是我一直到如今还怀恨这个泽明。

　　"我们驶了一星期才走到雅穆斯码头，然后我们遇到狂风——二十二年前有名的十月狂风。那是风、电、冰片、雪花合在一起，海里波涛涌得可怕。我们的船因为太轻就飞漂着，你们可以猜想那是多么不妙，当我告诉你们上层甲板的船舷被打成碎片，船面同洪水一样。第二晚，它把沙包移到下风边，那时我们已被吹到多革海岸了。没有办法，我们只好拿着铲下去，试把船身弄平，我们就在那广大的船底里，阴森森像一个洞穴，油脂做的烛插在横梁上，闪烁发光，暴风在上面怒号，船斜倾着发狂似的颠簸；我们都在那里，泽明，船主，以及每个人，几乎站不住脚，干这掘墓的勾当，努力把满铲的湿沙掷到上风边。船每翻动一下，你能够在朦胧的光线里模糊见到人们摔跤同乱挥铲子。船里一个男仆（我们有两个）感于这个情境的怪异，哭得好似他的心要碎了。我们能够听到他在阴影里某处痛哭着。

"第三天暴风停住了，不久一只北方的拖船把我们捡起。我们从伦敦到泰因（泰恩河，河上有当时英国煤炭主要出口港——编辑注）一共花了十六天！当我们走到船坞，我们装货的时机已经过去了，他们拖我们到一个码头，在那里我们滞了一个月。卑尔太太（船主的名字是卑尔）从科尔拆斯忒来看这个老头子。她就住在船上。野鸡水手都走了，只剩下船员，一个男仆，同一个管事，他是黑人同白人生下的混血儿，他叫做亚伯拉罕。卑尔太太是个老妇人，满脸皱纹，而且是通红的，像冬天的苹果，她的身材却像个少女。她有一次瞧见我正在缝上一粒纽扣，她坚持要把我的一切汗衫修补好。这跟我所知道的住在上等快帆船上的船主太太的确有些不同。当我把许多汗衫拿去给她修补，她说：'袜子呢？我敢说，它们也需要补缀，约翰的——船主卑尔

的——东西现在都料理好了。我很想干些事情。'
愿上帝祝福这个老妇人。她把我的行装替我详细
检查缝缮过，那时候我第一次读《衣裳哲学》同
柏那比的《基发骑行记》。前一本书我不大懂得，
但是我记得我喜欢兵士过于哲学家；我后来对于
人生的体验更证实了这个偏爱。一个是具有人性
的人，那一个是超过人性的——或者低于人性
的。然而，他们两位都死了，卑尔太太也死了，
青春，体力，天才，思想，成功，单纯的心——
这一切都死了；……不要紧。

　　"他们最后把我们这只船也装上货了。我们
雇了一队水手。八个能干的水手同两个男仆。一
天晚上我们驶开到船坞门口的浮标旁边，预备出
去，有个很好的希望，明天可以开始航行。卑尔
太太将搭晚车动身回家。当船泊好时，我们去用
茶点。吃的时候我们都不大说话——马洪，老夫
妇，同我。我先吃完，溜出去抽烟，我的卧室是
在甲板室里，刚靠着船尾楼。正是满潮时候，新
鲜的海风夹些微雨飞来；船坞的双重门开着，运
煤的汽船在黑暗中来来往往，他们的灯明亮地照
着，螺旋推进机溅水发出大声，绞车也嘎嘎作

响，码头上有许多呼唤的声音。我注视夜间在高处寂然滑过的一排头灯同在低处寂然滑过的一排绿灯，那时忽然间一线红光向我闪映，立刻隐没了，又看得见，就老滞在那儿。一只汽船的前头涌现在近旁。我向下面船员寝室喊道：'上来，赶快！'然后听到有个惊愕的声音在远处暗中说：'把它停住，先生。'一阵铃响。又一个声音警告地喊道：'我们将一直穿到那只帆船里去了，先生。'这句的回答是个粗暴的：'好了！'过一下子就是个沉重的撞击，当这个汽船的船头峭壁跟我们的齿轮擦过去地碰一下。接着就是暂时的纷乱，呼号同奔跑。蒸汽咆哮起来。然后听到一个人说：'全离开了，先生'……'你没有碰坏吗？'那个粗暴的声音问道。我跳到前面去瞧一下所受伤害，向他喊道：'我想大概没有。''慢慢向后退，'那个粗暴声音又说道。一阵铃响。'那是什么汽船？'马洪尖声问道。这时候它对于我们不过是一个庞大的影子设法驶走一些路了。他们向我们喊出一个名字——一个女人的名字，米兰大或者麦力萨——或者这类其他的名字。'这么一来，在这个兽窟一样的洞里还得滞一个月，'马

洪对我说，当我提着灯细看破碎的上层甲板船舷同冲断的舵轴，'但是船主在哪儿呢？'

"我们这些时候一点也没有听见他同看到他。我们到船尾去看。一个悲哀的高呼从船坞中间某处出来，'犹太，来呀！'……他怎样会鬼混到那里去呢？'唔？'我们叫喊。'我在我们的小船里漂流，没有桨了，'他说。一个在外面滞到太迟了来不及回家的船夫愿意帮忙，马洪同他商好给他半块银币把我们船主拖过来；但是先走上梯子的却是卑尔太太。他们于这轻寒的零雨之下在船坞里差不多漂荡了一个钟头。我一生里没有这么惊愕过。

"事情的经过是如此：当他听到我喊：'上来，'他立刻知道是什么事，抓起他的妻子，跳上甲板，跑过去，走到我们的小船，那是缚在梯边。六十老翁能够这么灵活也算难得了。请你们想一想这个老汉英雄地双手救起这个老妇人——他一生里最宝贵的女人。他把她放在坐板上，正预备跑回到船上去，船头系船的绳索却落下，他们就一同漂去了。当然在纷乱之中我们没有听到他的叫喊。他现出赧然的神气。她高兴地说：

'我想现在我赶不上火车也不要紧了。''不，真妮——你到下面去，那里暖和些，'他含怨说道。然后向我们说：'一个海员不该有个妻子——我说。你看我却到船外去了。好罢，这次没有什么大损伤。让我们去看这条傻汽船打坏了什么。'

"那并不是大损坏，但是使我们又迟留了三星期。这时期终止时候，船主跟他的经理们接洽事情，我拿卑尔太太的旅行囊到火车站，将她很舒服地安顿在三等车中。她把窗门扯下向我说：'你是个好青年。若使你看见约翰——卑尔船主——夜里没有用围巾，请你向他提一声，说我吩咐他脖子要好好包起。''一定的，卑尔太太，'我说。'你是个好青年，我看出你多么留心照呼约翰——船主……'火车忽然开走了，我对这个老妇人脱帽，我再也没看见她了……请把酒瓶递过来。

"我们第二天驶进海里去。当我们这下开始向盘谷航行，我们离伦敦已有三个月了。我们起先以为顶不过两星期左右的时光。

"那是正月，天气佳美——那种和煦有阳光的冬天日子，比夏天的更妙得多，因为那是出乎意料之外的，轻脆的，你又知道那不会，那不能继续很久。那好像是一笔横财，好像上帝赏赐的好东西，好像是一下意外的幸运。

"这种天气一直维持到北海，到海峡；一直维持到我们在利查底西面三百里左右的地方；然后转个风势，刮起东南风了。两天内成为暴风。犹太随波浮沉，在大西洋中打滚，像一只旧洋烛箱子。天天有暴风；含着憎恶地，不停地，毫无慈悲地，一下子也不歇息地刮着。世界无非是一大片打出白沫的大浪向我们冲来，上面的天低得伸手可触，龌龊得像个烟熏的天花板。我们四围的狂风雨里飞舞的浪花同空气一样的多。天天夜夜船的四旁没有别的，只是风的啸号，海的骚动，水倾泻到船面时的嘈杂。船是没有一刻的休息，我们也没有一刻的休息。它颠簸，它竖起，它倒栽，它坐在尾巴上，它滚动，它呻吟，我们在船面时就得抓住东西，在底下时就得依着寝棚，身体总是用力，心里总是焦虑。

"一天晚上马洪从我卧室的小窗子对我说话。那正朝着我睡的床铺，我躺在那里睡不着，穿着长靴，觉得我好像有许多年没有睡过，若使去试睡，也办不到。他兴奋地说道：

　　"'你这里有测水尺吗，马罗？我无法使抽水机吸水。天啊！这绝不是儿戏。'

　　"拿一把测水尺给它，又躺下来，打算去想些其他事情——但是我老想着那抽水机。当我走上船面，他们还在抽水机旁边努力工作，我当值时间到了，就同他们调班。靠着带到船面来看测水尺的灯笼的光线，我瞥见他们疲倦严重的脸孔。我们抽了整整四个钟头，整天，整个星期，我们轮班接连抽着。它自己渐渐松散了，漏水很多——没有多到会立刻将我们汹死，却足以让抽水工作累死我们。当我们抽水时候，船是一块一块地离散了；上层甲板的船舷去了，直杆也给风吹跑了，通气筒打成粉碎，房门也冲开了。船里没有一块干燥的地方。它的肠脏也是一块一块地被取出。一只长方形的船好像受了魔力变成为木片，它就站在上面受绞肠的苦痛。我自己也会鞭挞过它，我都还喜欢我的手艺，那能够这么久阻挡海的恶意。我们老是抽水。天气一些也没有改变。海是白得像一片白沫，像一锅煮滚的牛乳；密云没有一些破晴，不——连一手掌大的晴空都没有——不，连十秒钟的好天气都没有。对于我们可以说没有天，没有星，没有太阳，没有宇宙——什么都没有，除开盛怒的云同疯狂的海。我叫轮班抽水，为着要救我们这可爱的生命：这个工作仿佛继续了好几个月，好几年，永久继续着的，好像我们死过去，到地狱当水手了。我们忘却当下是星期几，我们忘却月名，我们忘却是何年，我们也不知道我们曾经住过岸上没有。帆吹掉了，它斜躺着，盖着油布，海倾泻到它上面，我们也不去理。我们只是转动抽水机的柄，眼神同傻子一样。我们一爬到船面，我常用一根绳把人、抽水机同主桅圈在一起，我们转动，不停地转动，水到我们腰间，到我们颈部，过我们的头了。这于我们还是一样的。我们早已忘却干的感觉是怎么样了。

"我心中隐隐想着：哈哈！这真是个怪有意思的冒险——活像你在书里所念的；这又是我第一次当二副的航行——我才二十二岁——此刻我也能挨着，不下于任何人，而且也使这班水手们照常工作。我感到愉快。我绝不肯抛弃这个经验，就算拿整个世界来给我换。我有狂欢的时候。每次这只裸露的小船使劲地竖起来，它的后尾高举在空中，由我看来，它好像把它船尾上所写的字'犹太，伦敦，工作，否则灭亡'扔上去，常做个恳求，当做个挑衅，当做个向毫无慈悲的云团的叫喊。

"呵，青春！它的力气，它的信仰，它的想象力！对于我，它并不是个发出嘎嘎声音的破旧东西，为着运费载一大堆煤在世界上跑来跑去——对于我，它是人生的努力，人生的试验，人生的磨练。我现在想起它时，还带有欣欢，带有感情，带有惋惜——正好似你想起一个你曾爱过的已死的人。我绝不会忘记它……请把酒瓶递过来。

"一天晚上，像我前面所说的，缚在主桅旁边，我们正在抽水，给风声弄聋了，没有精神到无力去希望自己是个死人，一阵波涛磅礴而来，冲到船面，把我们洗一遍。我一有力气呼吸，就按照我的责任喊道：'坚持到底，孩子们！'那时我忽然觉得一件浮在船面的硬东西打我的小腿。我去攫取，却没有抓到手。你们知道——四面是黑得一尺之内我们不能看清彼此的脸孔。

　　"这下砰击之后，船安稳了一会儿，那个东西，不管它是什么东西，又打我的小腿。这一回给我拿住了——那是一只汤锅。起先，因为我疲累得傻了，心里又只想那抽水机，我不知道我手里拿的是什么。忽然间，我明白了，我喊道：'孩子们，甲板室去了。离开这个工作罢，让我们去看厨子怎么样？'

　　"船的前头有一所甲板室，包含厨房，厨子的寝棚，同水手的住所。因为我们已经有好几天就预料出会看见它被水冲去，所以叫水手们到下面房间去睡——那是船里唯一安全的地方。我们的管事亚伯拉罕却偏要依恋他的寝棚，愚蠢地，像一只驴子——我相信完全出于恐惧，像一只牲口地震时不肯离开快坍下的兽栏。我们于是去看他。这是拿生命去冒险，因为一离开我们的捆绑，我们毫无掩护，正同在筏子上面一样。可是我们去了。那间屋子成为粉碎，好像一粒炸弹在里面爆发了。一大半东西都掉海里去了——炉子，人们的宿所，他们的财产，全掉海里去；但是扶着一部分船舱的间壁却留有两根柱子。大有神迹的意味，亚伯拉罕的床架就钉在上面。我们在遗迹之中摸索，碰到这个，他就在那里，坐床架上，四围是白沫同残物，高兴地向自己喃喃。他是神经错乱了，完全而且永久疯了，因为这个突然的惊骇刚乘着他忍耐到无可再忍的时候。我们把他捡起，强拽他到船尾，将他倒栽地扔给下面房子里的人们。你们知道我们没有时间去非常小心抬他下去，再等候着看他的情形有何变化。在下面的人们当然会在楼梯底将他拖起，一点儿也不错。我们是赶快跑回抽水机那里去工作。那件事是不能等待我们的。一个坏漏是个不近人情的东西。

"人们会以为这回魔鬼般的狂风的唯一目的是要把这可怜的管事弄疯。还不到天亮，风势就已平下了，第二天，天也明朗起来，海既然平静下去，漏口也自己塞住了。当我们安上一套新的帆，水手们要求驶回去——的确没有别的办法。小船都吹掉了，船面给水洗得空无一物，下面的房子内部也破坏得不堪，人们除开身上穿的之外没有一丝的衣服，粮食损失了，船身也过劳了。我们转过船头，向家乡驶去——你们会相信吗？现在却刮起东风，正是我们的对头风。它重新刮起来，而且是不停地。每走一时的路程，我们都得很费劲，但是它没有漏那么厉害了，水的呜咽也比较和平些。四个钟头中间得抽水两个钟头，这真不是开玩笑的事情——但是这样子它居然在水面挣扎到法尔马司。

　　"那里的善良住民是靠海上的灾难为生，看见我们一定是很高兴的。一群饥饿的造船匠瞧到这只死尸般的破船，赶紧磨利他们的凿子。天呀，在他们工作完了之前，的确骗了我们不少的钱。我想船的所有者已经很窘迫了。种种的停搁使它多滞了许久。然后决定把一部分的货运出，将它的干舷重新钉铁。这做完了，一切修理都已竣工，货也再运上去；一班新雇的水手上船，我们又扬帆到——盘谷，过了一星期，我们又回来。水手说他们不肯到盘谷——那有一百五十天的路程——在一只二十四个钟头里要抽水八个钟头的像两桅船的破船里；航海日报又登上这一小段新闻：'犹太，三桅船，自泰因到盘谷；煤；回到法尔马司，因为漏水同水手不肯服务。'

　　"又耽搁了许多——又修补一番。船的所有者来住一天，说它一点毛病也没有，简直像一架

小提琴。可怜的卑尔老船主憔悴不堪，活像一只
煤船船主的鬼——因为经过了这些忧虑同耻辱。
请你们记住他已六十岁了，这是他第一次带船。
马洪说这是一回无聊的事情，准会有个不好的结
果。我比从前更喜欢这条船，非常想到盘谷去。
到盘谷去！神秘的名字，幸福的名字。美索不达
米绝对比不上它。请记住我才二十岁，这是我第
一次得到二副的任命状，东方正在等候着我。

　　"我们驶出去，泊在外面码头，有一班新雇
的水手——第三班的。它漏水比从前更厉害。真
好像这班该死的造船匠的确在它上面打一个洞。
这一次我们简直没有驶出海口。水手根本就不肯
去料理绞盘。

　　"他们又把我们拖到内港里去，我们变为那
地方的一个固定物，一个景色，一个名胜了。人
们指出给游客看，说道：'这就是到盘谷去的那
只三桅船——在这里已经六个月了——回来三
次。'放假的日子，小孩子摇着小船，会喊道：
'犹太，唔！'若使有一个人在栏杆上露出头来，
他们会喊道：'你们到哪里去？——盘谷吗？'嘲
笑了一番。我们只有三个人在船上。可怜的老船

主在下面房间徘徊踯躅。马洪去当厨子，出人意
表地现出法国人做精美小菜的一切天才。我百无
聊赖地照料船缆。我们变为法尔马司的市民。个
个开店铺的人们都认得我们。在理发店或者烟铺
里，他们亲密地问道：'你想你真会到盘谷吗？'
当时，船的所有者，保险商，雇船者在伦敦彼此
争吵着，我们的薪水继续下去……请把酒瓶递
过来。

　　"这真是可怕。在精神方面，这比为着要救
自己生命而抽水还坏。仿佛我们被世界忘却了，
不属于谁的，也不会驶到任何地方；好像给魔力
所迷，我们不得不永久住在这个内港里，做一代
一代在长海岸上游手好闲的人们同不老实的船夫
的嘲弄材料和笑柄。我只三个月薪水，告了五天
假，跑到伦敦去。去的路程费了一天，回来的路
程差不多也费了一天——可是三个月的薪水仍然
是用光了。我不知道怎样花去。我相信，我到
游戏场去，在里真街上一家华美的馆子里用小
吃，用大餐，用午餐，刚好赶回来，没有带了别
的，只有一套《拜伦全集》同一副新旅行囊，算
做我三个月工作的成绩。渡我到大船去的船夫

说：'唔！我起先还以为你离开那家伙了。它绝不会驶到盘谷。''你只知道这些，'我轻蔑地说道——但是我心里非常不高兴这个预言。

"忽然间有一个人，某人的某一种代表。带了全权而来。他满脸都是酒齄，有种不屈挠的魅力，是个嘻嘻哈哈的人。我们又生气勃勃起来。一只旧船来到船旁，搬去我们的货，然后我们到干船坞，将我们船的铜皮剥下。它会漏水真是不足奇的。这个可怜东西，给暴风摧残到忍无可忍了，好像不胜厌恶，把它夹板缝里的填塞物都吐出来。它重新钉过铁，新包上一层铜皮，弄得坚固得像一只瓶子。我们回到旧船，把货又搬回来。

"然后，一个良好的月夜，所有耗子都离开这只船了。

"我们一向受它们的骚扰。它们咬坏我们的帆布，吃我们的粮食比水手还厉害，殷勤地与我们同床，患难相共，现在当这只船可以航海了，却决定离开。我叫马洪来赏玩这个奇观。耗子跟着耗子现在我们栏杆上，从肩上回头作最后一顾，空洞地'砰'的一声掉到破旧的空船里。我们想去数它们，但是一会儿就数乱了。马洪说：
'好罢！别同我说耗子是多么聪明。它们从前该
离开，当我们万分危险，几乎沉没了。现在你有
个证明，可以看出关于它们的迷信是多么无谓。
它们离一只好船，到一个老朽的旧船，那里什么
吃的都没有，这是傻瓜！……我不相信它们比你
我更知道什么是他们的安全，和什么事于它们有
好处。'

　　"又谈论了一下子，我们公认耗子的智慧是
太称赞过分了，其实并不比人们的高明多少。

　　"这只船的遭遇这样子从兰斯恩德一直到福
耳兰这条海峡的人们都知道了，我们从南海岸无
法雇到水手。他们从利物浦送一全班水手来，我
们又出发——到盘谷去。

　　"我们风平浪静，一直驶到热带，这条老船
犹太就在阳光之下行步艰难地望前进。当它每小
时走八里时，上面的一切东西都响起来，好像将
折断了，我们把小帽紧缚在头上；但是它常是每
小时走三里，慢慢溜着。你们怎能期望它不是这
样呢？它是疲倦了——这只老船。它的青春正同
我的青春一样，是已过去了——也正同你们的青

春一样，你们诸位听这个故事的先生们。有哪位
朋友肯当面说你们年纪太大，或者太疲劳了呢？
我们并不责备它。最少，在我们住在船尾的官员
眼里，好像我们是生于斯，长于斯，在这里面住
了许多年头了，仿佛绝没有知道过别只船。我不
打算骂它，正如我不会因为家乡的老礼拜堂不是
个大教堂，就去说它的坏话。

　　"至于我，我的青春也使我更有耐心。在我
的前途有整个的东方同一切的生活，想到在这只
船上我遇到磨折，居然对付得很不错，我更觉得
高兴。我就想起古代的人们，他们几世纪以前坐
着并不更高明的船，也走这条航路，到棕树（棕
榈树——编辑注）、香料同黄沙的国土，那里有
棕色种的人民，他们的皇帝比罗马的尼罗王更残
酷，比犹太的所罗门更奢华。老船还是步履蹒跚
地望前走，因为上了年纪同载了货物变得很沉
重了，我却是在无知识同热烈希望里度青春的生
活。它步履蹒跚地望前走，一天又一天，好像永
无止期；在落照之下反映出的新涂泥金好像向
这将螟的大海喊出尽在它船尾的几个字：'犹太，
伦敦，工作，否则灭亡。'

"然后，我们驶进印度洋，望北朝着爪哇·赫德走去。海上只有微风。一星期一星期过去了。它还是慢爬着，努力否则灭亡，家乡的人们开始打算出布告，说我们过期未到。

"一天星期六黄昏时候，我正在休息，水手们请我给他们另外一桶左右的水——为着洗衣服用。我不愿意这么迟还去扭上淡水唧筒（水泵——编辑注），就吹着哨子往前走，手里拿一把钥匙去打开船头舱的舱口，想从我们放在里面的一个多余的水柜取水。

"下面的臭味真是出乎意料的，真是可怕。闻到这臭味，人们会以为有一百枝白蜡灯在那个洞里吐焰熏烟了许多日子。我走出来，如释重负。跟我同去的人咳嗽说道：'怪味，先生。'我不留心地答道：'据说这于身体有益，'走向船尾去了。

"我第一件干的事情是低下头，伸进船中间气筒的方口。当我揭开那盖子，一些看得见的敢，有点像薄雾，一阵细微的烟雾，从口里出来。上升的气是热的，有一种浓厚的，烟煤的，白蜡的臭味。我只闻一下，就轻轻地把盖子关上。把我自己弄得窒息是没有用的。下面的货物分明是燃烧起来了。

"第二天，它真真冒出烟来。你们看这是在意料之内的，虽然所运的煤是属于安全那一种的，可是这些货搬来搬去，搬的时候又弄得这么碎，看起来，它不像别的，简直像铁匠铺的煤块。后来又浸了水——还不止一次。当我们把它从破旧的空船取回，天老是下雨，现在走了这么长的路程，它发热了，这又是自然燃烧的一个例子。

"船主叫我们到他的房间。他有一张地图铺在桌面，现在忧愁的神气。他说：'西澳大利亚海岸离这儿不远，但是我想向我们的目的地走去。这又是暴风的月令；但是我们决定使船头朝着盘谷，跟火奋斗。绝不再回转去停泊在任何地方了，就说我们都烤焦了。我们要先用缺乏空气来熄灭这个倒霉的燃烧。'

"我们尝试一下。我们拿一切东西去喂它，它仍然冒烟。烟老是从看不见的裂缝出来；它由船舱的间壁同船面的盖布冲透出来；它一丝丝地这里，那里，到处泄漏出来，一片薄雾，怎么能够跑出真是不可思议。它走进房间里面，走到船头甲板；它使船面有遮盖的地方也染上毒气，甚至于大帆顶上也闻得出它烟味。若使烟能走出，那么空气分明能够进去。这叫我们寒心。这个燃烧不肯熄灭。

　　"我们决定用水来试一试，将货仓口打开，一阵阵大卷的烟，白色的，黄色的，浓厚的，油腻的，雾一般的，使人不能通气的，上升一直到桅顶的木球。一切人们都躲到船尾去。然后，这阵毒云吹走了，我们回去工作，四围的烟现在只有普通烟囱的烟那么深厚了。

　　"我们装好压水唧筒，接上水龙软管，可是软管渐渐破裂了。唉，那是跟这只船同样老——一个前史时的水龙软管，已是无法修补了。我们于是就用微弱的抽水筒，拿桶子来盛水，这样子设法及时将好些印度洋的水灌到货舱大仓口。明亮的海水在太阳光中发光，倾泻到一层慢爬着的白烟里去，就消失于煤块的黑色表面上了。蒸汽混着烟一同上来。我们好像将盐水灌注一个无底的大桶。这是我们的命运，在这只船里抽水，把水从船里抽出，又从外面抽水到船底去；从前使船里没有水，免得我们沤死，我们现在却疯狂地灌水进去，救我们自己，免得烧死。

"它却迟缓地望前爬，努力，否则灭亡，在恬静的天气里。天是洁净得出奇，蓝蔚得出奇。海是光滑的，澄蓝的，透明的，发光像一粒宝石，向四面伸长，一直到天边——仿佛地球是一粒钻石，一粒大碧玉，一粒宝石造成的行星。在这没有风波的大海里，犹太偷偷地溜走，有沉闷不洁的烟雾包着，藏在徐行的云里，那向下风处飘去，轻轻的，慢慢的；这是一阵含有毒质的云，把海天的光荣弄脏。

"这些时候里我们自然没有看见火。货在底下某处冒着烟。有一回，马洪，当我们站在一排工作时候，现出一种古怪的笑容，向我说道：'吓，若使它此刻会生一个刚合式的漏口——像我们第一次离开海峡时候那样——就可以把这阵火止着了。你看会不会？'我所答非所问地说道：'你记得耗子吗？'

"我们跟火奋斗，小心地驶船，仿佛并没有什么意外事情发生。管事在厨房里煮菜，伺候我们。其余十二人，八个工作，四个休息。每个人轮班，船主也在内。真是平等，虽然不能严格地说有友爱，可是彼此都很怀有好感。有时一个人，当他倒满桶的水到舱口里去，会喊道：'哈哈，到盘谷去！'其他人们就大笑起来。但是通常我们是静默同严肃——而且口渴。啊，多么渴呀！我们又不敢随便用水。严格的限制，船冒着烟，太阳是灼热的……把酒瓶递过来罢。

"我们试尽了一切法子。我们甚至于想掘到发火的地方。这当然是办不到的。没有一个人能够在底下滞过一分钟。马洪第一个下去，晕倒在那里，去救他出来的人也晕倒了。我们把他们强拽出来，放在船面上，然后，我跳下去，为的是给他们看这是多么容易办到的。他们现在学乖了，只用链钩缚住，我相信是，寻柄上把把我钩起来。我也不愿意再下去捡起我的铲子，那就滞在下面。

"情形有些不妙了。我们将长艇放到水里去。第二条艇我们也预备让它去随潮旋转。我们还有一只，十四英尺长的小艇，挂在船尾吊艇架上，那是很安全的。

"然后，你们看，烟忽然间减少了。我们加

倍我们的力量去灌船底。两天后，一点烟也没有了。每个人都笑逐颜开。这是星期五的事情。星期六不做什么工作，船当然还是照常驶着。人们两星期来第一次洗净他们的衣服同脸孔，享受一顿特别丰富的大餐。他们谈到天然燃烧时现出蔑视，隐含着他们是扑灭天然燃烧的好汉这个意思。我们都觉得仿佛承受了一笔大财产。但是有一种可厌的焦味回绕船中。卑尔船主双目凹下，脸颊陷进去。我从前绝没有注意到他的身体是这么扭歪弯曲。他同马洪严肃地在舱口同通气筒旁边考察，伸着鼻子闻。我忽然觉得可怜的马洪是个非常非常老的汉子。至于我自己，我是骄傲高兴，好像我出力打胜一仗大海战。呵！青春！

"夜是佳美的。早上，有一只回国的船从我们道上经过，船身隐于水平线下，只看得见帆樯——这是好几月来我们第一次遇见的船；但是我们终于走近目的地了。跟爪哇·赫德只隔一百九十里，差不多一直望着北方走。

"第二天从八时到十二时是我在船面轮班的时候。早餐时候，船主说：'真奇怪，那种味老缠在船上房间里面。'十点时候，大副在船尾甲板上，我走下到中甲板滞一会儿。木匠的长凳站在中桅旁边；我靠着它，一面抽我的烟斗，木匠，一个年青的人，来同我闲谈。他说：'我想我们干得不坏，是不是？'然后我心里有些不愉快，看到这个傻家伙想把这长凳踢走。我不客气地说道：'不要这样，木匠，'立刻有一个奇怪的感觉，一个荒谬的幻觉——我好像到空中去了。我听见四围仿佛有一个闭住的气息松吐出来——好像一千位巨人同时喊一声'孚！'——感到一个沉闷的打击，那使我的肋骨忽然痛起来。这是无可疑的——我是在空中，我的身体正画一条短抛物线。但是虽然很短，我还有时间想几个念头，就我记忆所及，大概是底下这样一个次序：'这不是木匠捣乱——是什么呢？一些意外的事变——海底火山吗？——煤，煤气！——哈哈！我们的船爆发了——个个人都死了——我掉到后货舱舱口—— 看见里面的火。'

"货舱空中浮动的煤层当爆发时候呈出暗红色的光辉。一刹那间，从长凳被踢后一秒钟的几千万万分之一的时间之内，我已全身爬在货上面了。我自己站起，赶紧跑出来。那是快得有如反响。船面是一片碎木的旷野，交叉躺着，像狂风后的森林；一块非常大的坚固烂幕布在我们面前飘荡——那是扯成碎条的大帆。我想，樯桅立刻会倒下，为着免受伤，我突然双手双脚爬到船尾甲板的楼梯旁。我第一个看见的人是马洪，眼睛同碟子一样大，嘴张开着，长的白发一根一根直着站在他头上，像银色的灵光。他正要走下来，看见中甲板蠢动，掀起，在他眼前变成碎片，却把他吓住了，木鸡般站在楼梯最高那一格上。我不相信地瞧着他，他也带个古怪的惊骇的好奇盯着我。我自己不知道我没有头发，没有眉毛，没有睫毛，我年青的髭须烧掉了，我的脸孔是墨黑的，一边脸颊破了，我的下巴流血。我遗失了我的帽子，一只拖鞋，我的汗衫也扯成碎布了。这许多情形我都不晓得。我很惊奇，看到船还是浮着，船尾甲板还是整个——尤其看到还有人活着。海天的恬静也是很惊异的。我想我预料会看见他们吓得抽筋……请把酒瓶递过来。

　　"有一个声音，喊我们船名，从某处发出——从空中呢，从天上呢——我说不清。我立刻看见船主——他是疯了。他热烈地问我：'房里的桌子到哪里去了？'听见人家问这样一句话，神经还为着这个经验而颤动，——我还没有十分把握，我自己是否活着。马洪顿起双脚来，向他喊道：'天呀！你还不知道船面冲掉了吗？'我能发出声音了，结巴地说道，好像觉得自己有很大的失职：'我不晓得房里桌子跑哪里去。'这活像一场荒谬的狂梦。

　　"你们猜得出他接着要干什么吗？他要我们调整帆桁。很沉静地，好像浸在默想里面，他坚持把帆桁跟桅樯成为直角。'我不知道船上还有人活着没有，'马洪说，差不多是含泪地。'可是，'他温和地答道，'剩下的人们总够调整帆桁。'

　　"这个老头子好像正在他床铺上开时计，这个打击使他颠旋房里。他立刻想到——他后来说——船碰到什么东西了，就跑到外面房间去。那里他看见房间的桌子消失得不知去向。船面既然炸飞，这当然也流落到船尾积物室里去了。那天我们用早餐的地方，他现在只看见地板上一个大窟窿。这件事他觉得这么神秘可怕，这样深刻地感动了他，他到船面后的所见所闻跟这个一比较，都成为无关紧要的细事了。你们看，他立刻注意到舵轮没有人管，他的船离开它的航路了——他唯一的观念是使这个可怜的，裸体的，无甲板的，冒烟的船壳还是朝着它的目的地走去。向盘谷开驶！这是他所想办的。我告诉你们这个恬静驼背，腿向外弯，差不多可以算做残缺的矮小老头子，他观念的古怪同他毫不慌张地不了解我们的震惊真是有些过度。他用一种命令的姿势指挥我们望前工作，他自己去管舵轮。

"是的，这是我们所干的第一件事情——调整这个破船的帆桁！一个人也没有死，甚至于没有一个人成为残疾人，但是每人多少受些损伤。你们真该瞧见我们当时的情形！有些穿着破烂的衣服，脸孔黑得同运煤夫的一样，简直像扫烟囱的人，头小得有如弹丸，那好像剃光了，其实是烧到头皮。其他在下面的船员因为寝棚塌了，被扔出来而惊醒，不断地颤抖，甚至于我们工作时候，还在那儿呻吟。但是他们都做工。这班利物浦的硬汉身里有真正的好气质。这是我的经验，他们总是如此。海——他们蒙昧灵魂四围的空旷同寂寞，赋他们以这个性质。吓！我们摔跤，我们爬动，我们的胫骨触着破碎木头擦去踵皮，我们拖扯东西。桅樯站着，但是我们不知道它们底下烧焦了多少。天气差不多是恬静的，但是一阵浪涌从西方来，使它转动。那些桅樯随时可以颠覆。我们恐惧地望着它们。人们无法预料它们会向哪面倒下。

"然后我们退到船尾去，看一看四面的情境。船面是破板，零段，碎片同毁坏的木头家伙的堆积所。桅樯从这混乱的杂物里抽出，好像大树从密生的矮林里伸出。这堆破烂物的空隙满是一种白色蠕动的东西——同油腻的雾差不多。看不见的火的烟又上升了，回绕着，有如充塞于朽木的山谷里浓密的毒雾。已经有些慢飘的鬼火开始从这杂碎里望上蜿蜒。这儿那儿有些木头壁直插着，像一根柱子。围桅的栏杆一半穿到前樯的纵帆里去，天空在这沾污的难看的帆布破处现出一块光荣的蓝色。几块架在一起的木板有一部分横在标杆外面，一头突出船外，像一个到虚空去的舷门，像一个到深海去的舷门，引我们走上死路——好像请我们立刻去跳板，将我们这可笑的麻烦结束。在空中，在天上——仿佛有个精灵，一个看不见的东西叫我们的船名。

"有人倒晓得向船外望一下，看见我们的舵工，他起先一时冲动跳到海里去，焦急地想回来。他大声喊叫，很带劲地浮水，像一条人鱼，总在船旁边，不敢落后。我们抛一条绳子给他，他立刻站在我们中间，水同江河一样从他身上流下，很垂头丧气的样子。船主也不理那舵轮了，独自在一处，肘倚着栏杆，手支着颐，黯然凝视着海。我们问自己道：'再会有什么事情呢？'我想，这才像冒险，这真是伟大。我纳罕着会有什么事情发生。啊，青春！

"忽然间马洪瞧见一条汽船远在船后。卑尔船主说：'我们还可以向它去设法。'我们挂起两面旗，那用海洋上的世界语说：'着火，需急救。'汽船很快就变大了，渐渐也在前桅上挂两面旗，旗语的意思是：'我正来救你。'

"半点钟内，它同我们居在同一行列上，在上风那一边，彼此相喊听得见，微微颤簸着，它的机器停住。我们失掉了镇静，齐声激昂地喊道：'我们被火冲飞了。'一个戴白色窄边拿破仑式帽子的人站在舰桥上喊：'是的！不要紧！不要紧！’他点头微笑，用手做安慰的姿势，好像对着一群吓了的小孩子。一只小船下水，荡它的长桨向我们走来。四个加拿士（Calashes）人轻快地划来。这是我第一次见到马来水手。此后我很知道他们，那时使我觉得奇怪的是他们的不关心：他们来到旁边，甚至于站起，拿船钩搭在我们的大铁链上面的划头桨的人也不肯赏脸抬头望我们一眼。我心里想被火冲到天上去的人们总值得受更大的注意。

　　“一个矮小汉子，干枯像根木屑，活泼像只猴子，爬上来。这是汽船的大副。他看了一眼，就说道：‘呵，孩子们——你们还是离开这只船好些罢。’

　　“我们都默然，他独自跟船主谈一会儿，——仿佛是跟他辩论。然后他们一同上汽船去。

　　“当我们船主回来，我们听他说这只汽船叫做散麦维尔，船主是那士，从西澳大利亚到新加坡去，路过巴塔菲亚，带有邮件，我们订的合同是它拖我们到盘革，假使可能，就到巴塔菲亚，在那里我们可以在船侧打一个孔把火弄灭，然后继续我们的航程——到盘谷去！老头子好像兴奋起来。'我们还要干下去，'也凶猛地向马洪说。
他握拳向天。别人不吭一声。

"中午时候汽船开始拖我们。它苗条高高地
在前面走，犹太这个残破的船在七十寻船缆的末
端跟着——轻快地跟它，像一团黑烟，桅杆的顶
露在上面。我们爬到帆索的高处去卷船帆。到帆
桁时我们咳嗽，到帆腹时非常小心。你们看见我
们这班人吗，仔细地卷起那命定了永不会抵任何
地方的船的帆？个个人都认为随时桅樯会倾覆下
来。从上面，我们只见烟，看不见船，他们小
心地工作，好好地接连着传递束帆索。'向港口
卷去——你们这班在上面的人们！'马洪从底下
喊道。

"你们懂得这一点吗？我不相信这几个汉子
里面有一个预料会照通常的样子下来。当我们平
安着地了，我听见他们彼此说道：'呀，我起先
想我们将从船上掉到海中，一大堆的——木头
和我们一起——你可以骂我，假使我不是这样
想。''这正是我对自己想的，'另一个受伤了，
缚了绷带的憔悴的人疲倦地答道。请你们注意，
这班人并没有受过训练，养成服从习惯。在一个

旁观人眼里，他们是一群毫无虔信心境的流氓，绝没有什么好处。什么使他们工作——什么使他们服从我，当我自觉地想到这是多么有意思，叫他们一再放下前帆的帆腹，为的是要弄得牢靠些？什么呢？他们并没有职业上的荣誉——没有什么例子，也得不到赞美。这也不是出于他们的责任心；他们都很知道怎样躲懒偷闲——当他们想这样干的时候——他们多半都有这种念头。是不是因为叫他们来的这个每月二镑十先令的薪金呢？他们觉得他们该受一倍多的报酬，不；这是他们身里的性质，一些天生的，微妙的，永久的气氛。我并没有积极地说一只法国或者德国商船上的水手不能干这些事，但是，我怀疑他们会不会这样干。这里面有一种完美的态度，坚固得有如主义，能够驾驭一切有如本能——露出一些秘密的性质——一些隐晦的气氛，一种先天的善恶之分，那做成种族的差别，那铸定国家的命运。

"这是在那晚上十点钟，我们第一次看见火，自从我们跟它奋斗以来。拉牵的速度扇动了冒烟的烈火。一线绿光现于前面，照亮底下甲板上的残破情形。它变成小块火球摇动着，蠕动慢爬，像一只流萤的光。我先瞧见，告诉马洪。'那么失败了，'他说。'我们还是停止这个拉牵好罢，否则它会前后爆裂，在我们能够走开之前。'我们狂叫起来；摇铃引他们的注意；他们还是向前拖。末了，迫得马洪同我爬到前面，用一把斧头把绳子砍断。因为来不及去解绳索了。在我回到船尾的途中，我们看得见红火舌舐我们脚下的一片木屑的旷野。

"他们在汽轮上当然很快就发觉绳子断了，它的汽笛大叫一声，我们看船上的灯光飞快地兜个大圈子，它走来排在我们船旁，停住了。我们紧紧地挤成一团站在船尾甲板上，望着它。每个人手里都保留有一捆或者一包的东西。忽然一个带螺旋形顶的圆锥形火焰冲上天去，投一个光圈到黑海上面，这两只船并排在这个圈的中心轻轻起落着。卑尔船主坐在铁格上发呆有好几个钟头了，但是现在他慢慢站起来，走到我们前面，一直走到尾桅桅索上。那士船主喊道：'快些！当心点。我船上有邮包。我一定带你们同你们的小船到新加坡去。'

"'谢谢你！不！'我们船主说，'我们一定要

看这条船的究竟。'

　　"'我们不能在你们旁边了,'那个人喊道,
'邮包——你们知道。'

　　"'是!是!我们没有危险。'

　　"'好罢!我到新加坡时替你们报告……再
见!'

　　"他挥手告别。我们这班人们悄悄地落下手
里的包裹。汽船向前驶去,走出光圈,我们立刻
看不见他了,因为我们眼睛给燃烧得很凶猛的火
弄眩了。然后,我晓得我第一次瞧见东方时,我
将是个小艇的总指挥。我想这真妙;我们这样忠
于老船,我觉得也很妙。我们将看见它的究竟。
呵,青春的魔力!呵,青春的火焰,比着火的船
的火焰更来得令人目眩,射出有魔力的光辉到大
地上,大胆地跳到天上去,很快就给'时间'湮
没了,那是比海更残酷,更无怜悯,更苛刻——
跟着火的船的火焰一样,被坚不可破的黑夜吞没
进去了。

　　"老头子用他那温和而固执的口吻警告我们,
这是我们责任的一部分,尽力替保险商救出船上
的东西。于是乎我们到船尾去工作,它就在船头

大放光明，足以照我们做事情。我们拖出一大堆
废物。有什么我们不拿呢？一只陈旧的寒暑表，
没有道理地钉了无限多的钉子，几乎要了我的
命：一阵烟忽然冲来，我刚来得及躲闪。这里有
许多的物品，好几捆的帆布，好几圈的绳子，船
尾甲板看起来好像海洋物品的市场，小艇堆得满
到船沿。人们会以为这个老头子想从他第一次领
的船尽力带走许多东西。他是非常非常镇静，但
是分明是糊涂了。你们会相信吗？他要拿很长的
旧水线同一把小锚到他的长艇里去。我们恭敬地
答道："是的，是的，先生，'暗地里让这些东西
溜到海里去。一只沉重的医药箱也这样子消失
了，还有两袋绿咖啡，许多罐油漆——你们想一
想，油漆！——以及许多其他东西。然后，我得
到命令，同两个水手到这几只小艇去装货，把它
们弄好，预备我们该离大船的时候。

　　"我们把一切东西装好，替我们船主把长艇
的桅杆竖起，这条艇是将归他去负责的，我坐下
憩息一会儿，觉得松活一下。我的脸孔肿痛，四
肢疼得有如折断了，我感到一切肋骨的不舒服，
敢赌咒我的脊骨扭歪了。小艇紧靠在船尾，躺在

浓影之中，四面看得见一大圈海给火照亮。一阵
巨大的火焰从船前面清澈笔直地上升。它很猛烈
地闪燃，声音响得像羽翼的拍打，还有像雷声的
霹雳。此外杂有噼啪同轰发的声音，火花就从这
个圆锥形的火焰生出来望上飞，正像人为将来的
灾难，为漏水的船，为着火的船而生的那样。

　　"使我麻烦的是大船船舷朝着滚来的浪，对
着那时所有的风——一些的微风——以至小艇不
肯安居船尾，那里却是安全的地方；它们像小艇
们通常那种顽梗的样子，一定要跑到船尾突出
部的下面，然后摆到旁边去。它们危险地碰来
撞去，走近火焰，大船在它们上面滚转，自然
时时刻刻又有桅樯倒下的危险。我同两个守船
的人用船桨同船钩极力设法使它们离开大船；但
是老是卖这种力气真够令人愤怒，因为我们没有
可以滞留的理由。我们不能看见船上的人们，也
想不出什么产生了这耽搁。守船那两个人轻轻地
发誓，我不单有我分下的工作，还得注意这两个
人工作，他们常常表示出躺下让小艇顺流溜去的
倾向。

　　"末了，我喊道：'在船面的人们，'有一个

人望下瞧。'我们这里预备好了，'我说。那个头看不见了，很快又露出来。船主说：'很好，先生，不要使小艇靠近大船。'

"半点钟过去了。忽然间有一阵可怕的嘈杂，刮辣的声音，铁链的琅珰声，水的咝声，无数万的火花飞上，到颤动的烟柱里，那是稍微比船高一些，斜倚在那儿。徽章烧掉了，两个烧得通红的锚也跑到海底去了，扯着烧得通红的二百英寻铁链跟它下去。整个船颤动，那一团火挥舞，好像将塌陷，船首的上樯也就倒下了。它火箭似的投下，射到海里去，立刻跳出来，同小船只有一桨之距，安详地浮着，在明亮的海上显得非常黑。我又向船上喊。过了一会儿，一个人用一种出乎意料地高兴的，但是好像他想闭着嘴说话了。有许久时间，我只听到火的呼呼声同咆哮声。还有呜呜声。小船跳动着，拖拉它们的船缆，开玩笑地冲来冲去，船舷相碰，无论我们怎么办，总是一大堆摆到大船旁边。我不能再忍了，攀登一根绳子，从船尾爬到船上去。

"船面明亮得同白天一样。这样爬上去，对着我的这一片火光看起来真是可怕，那股热气起

先好像几乎无法忍受。一只有背睡椅的垫子，那
是从房里拖出的，卑尔船主坐在上面，他的双眼
弯起，一只臂给头枕着，正睡着，火光对着他闪
烁。你们知道其他人们忙着什么吗？他们坐在船
尾，围着一只打开的箱子，吃面包同酪饼，喝瓶
装的黑麦酒。

　　"凶猛火舌绞扭着在他们头上，他们对于这
样的背境觉得很舒适，同火蛇一样，活像一班不
顾性命的强盗。火在他们眼睛的白部发光，射到
他们破内衣所露出的一块一块白皮肤上。个个人
身上好像都有战争的痕迹——绷带缚着的头，扎
起来的手臂，一条龌龊的破布围着膝部——个个
人有一瓶酒夹在腿上，一厚块酪饼在手里。马洪
站起来。他那美丽而下流的头，那钩形的侧面，
那雪白的长胡子，他手里打开橡皮塞的瓶子，这
几点使他像古代不顾死生的海盗，在残忍同蹂躏
之中作乐。'我们在船上最后的一餐，'他严重地
声明。'我们整天没有东西吃，这些食物都留下
也是没有用的。'他挥舞他的瓶子，指着睡正浓
的船主。'他说他吃不下什么东西，所以我弄他
去躺下，'他继续说；当我直着眼睛看他，'我不

知道你晓得不晓得，年青的人，这个老头子有好多天没有睡了——将来在小艇里睡的机会也少得该咒。'‘将没有小艇了，若使你们再胡闹下去，’我生气地说。我走向船主，推他的肩膀。最后，他睁开眼睛，但是并不动。‘已到离开它的时候了，先生，’我镇静地说道。

"他满身疼痛地站起，看着火焰，看一看船四周发光的海，和再远黑得同墨水一样的海；他望一望星群，那是在黑得像地狱门的天空里一层稀薄的烟雾中蒙昧发光。

"‘最年青的先离船，’他说。

"普通水手用手背揩嘴，站起，爬过船尾栏杆，看不见了。别人跟着走。有一个正要跨过去，站住喝干他的酒瓶，手臂一挥，扔到火里去。‘把这个也拿去罢，’他喊道。

"船主悲哀地滞在后面，我们让他独自跟他第一次带的船默语一会儿。然后我又上去，末了把他引下。这真是该离船的时候了。船尾铁的东西触着感到火热。

"然后长艇的船缆割断，三只小船缚在一起，漂走远离大船了。我们舍弃它刚在它爆发后十六个钟头。第二条小艇归马洪负责，我管最小那一条——十四尺长的小艇。本来长艇就够载我们全部的人；但是船主说我们必得尽力救起船上财产——替保险商——这样子我第一次得到指挥权。我有两个人同我一起，一袋饼干，几罐肉，一小桶水。我得到命令，叫我紧靠着长艇，为的是天气恶劣时我们可以收留到长艇里去。

"你们知道我想什么吗？我想只要办得到，我就要同他们分手。我要独自占有这第一次得到的指挥权。假使有独自航行的机会，我是不肯整队前进的。我要凭着自己的本领把它带领靠岸。我要比其他船都走得快。青春！这全是青春！愚蠢的，可爱的，美丽的青春。

"但是我们并不立刻出发。我们一定要看这只船的空间。于是小艇那晚上就在旁边漂荡，随着浪涌而浮定。人们微睡，醒来，叹息，呻吟。我就望着火烧的大船。

"夹于海天的黑暗之中，它猛烈地烧着，在一圈给跳跃着的血红火光照成紫色的海面上；在一圈灿烂而阴险的水面上。一条明亮的高飞火焰，一条寂寞的极大火焰，由海里上升，从它的高巅有黑烟不断地向天空冲去。它暴怒地烧着；悲哀庄严得像火葬的积薪在夜里点燃，大海围绕着，星群注视着。一个堂皇的死仪像一个恩典，像一份礼物，像一件奖品，给这条老船，在他辛苦生涯的这个末日。它这疲劳的灵魂付给星群同大海去安排，这正同光荣的凯旋同样地感动人们。天将破晓时候，船桅倒下了，一下子火花四散乱飞，好像使耐心的，留神的夜，静默的卧在大海上的空旷的夜，满是飞火。天亮时，它只是一只烧焦的外壳，安详地在一阵烟云之下漂游，里面载有一堆白热的煤块。

　　"然后，船桨拿出来，小船成一条线围着它的遗留绕行，好像列队送葬——长艇带领着。当我们驶过船尾时，一朵苗条的火焰刻毒地向我们射来，它忽然间沉下，倒栽的，蒸汽很响地咝一声。尚未毁坏的船尾最后沉下去；但是油漆已经没有了，爆裂了，剥落了，船尾没有字母，没有什么话了，没有恍惚是它的灵魂的那倔强的铭语，对着上升的太阳，闪出它的信条同它的名字。

　　"我们望北走去。一阵微风吹起，将到中午

时候，一切小艇最后聚会一下子。我的小艇没有桡，也没有帆，但是我拿一根多余的桨做一根桡，挂上一个布帐当船帆，拿船钩做船桁。他的桡楢的确太重了，但是我心里高兴，知道靠着从船尾吹来的风，我能够追过其他两只船。我得等候它们。然后，我们看一下船主的地图，大家感情融洽地吃一顿硬面包同水，听到最后的训令。那是很简单的：望北走，尽力聚在一起行驶。'当心那个假桡，马罗，'船主说；马洪，当我骄傲地驶过他的小艇时候，皱起他那弯曲的鼻子，喊道：'你将在水底行舟，假使你不小心，年青的人。'他是个苛刻的老头子——希望他现在所长眠的大海轻轻地摇荡他，慈爱地摇荡他，一直到宇宙的末日！

"黄昏之前，一阵密密的暴风雨降到那两只小艇，它们是远在我这小船的后面，这次看见后，我就没有见到它们了，一直有好久时候。第二天，我坐着驶我这海壳般的轻舟——我第一次带领的船——四围没有别的，只是水天茫茫。下午我的确看见远处一只大船的上帆，但是我不吭一声，我的水手没有注意到。你们看我心里怕它是一只归帆，我却不想转身回去，没有进东方的大门。我是向爪哇驶去——那也是个快乐的名字——同盘谷一样，你们知道。我驶了许多日子。

"我用不着告诉你们在一只空船里颠簸是怎么样子。我记得许多日子整天整夜的全然无风，我们划桨，我们划桨，船却好像站住，仿佛给魔力迷惑了，不能走出水平线做成的这一圈海面。我记得酷热，暴风雨的泛滥，那使我们为着救这可爱的生命不断地用桶将船里的水汲出（但是灌满了我们的水瓶），我还记得接连十六个钟头口渴干得焦渣，一只舵桨在船尾上使我这第一次带领的船还能头朝着来浪山崩的大海。在那时候以前，我不知道我自己是个多么有本领的汉子。我记得我两个水手瘦长的脸孔同憔悴的样子，我记得我的青春，同那永不会再回来的感觉——当时我觉得我能够永久维持下去，比海，天，和一切人们都更耐久；就是这样一种骗人的感觉，引诱我们到欣欢，到危险，到爱情，到白费的努力——最后到死的途上去；这是优胜者对于自己力量的深信不疑，这是在这盈握的尘土做成的身

体里面的生命热气，这是我们心中的闪烁火光，
那却随年时而暗淡，而冷却，而消沉，终于熄灭
了——熄灭得真是太早，真是太早——还在生命
熄灭之前。

"这是我怎样见到东方。我曾经看见过它秘
密的地方，曾经深悉它的灵魂；但是现在我对于
东方的印象总是从一只小船，对面是一列高山，
在晨曦里蓝色的，辽远的；在中午时像一层薄
雾；在落照之下变成为紫色的凸凹不一的长墙。
我手里好像有一只桨，眼中好像看到灼热的碧
海。我还看见一个海湾，一个广阔的海湾，玻璃
一样的地平，结冰一样地滑，在黑暗中发微光。
一盏红灯远在陆地的幽暗里燃烧着，夜是温柔
的，暖和的。我们用酸痛的手臂荡桨，忽然间一
阵风，一阵带有花卉同香木的馨气的温暖微风，
从静寂的夜里吹来——这是东方向我第一下的叹
息。这是我永不会忘却的。这是不可捉摸的，迷
人的，像一种魔力，像向我们耳语，暗地里允许
了神秘的欣欢。

"我们这最后一次的荡舟一共花了十一个钟
头。两人划船，那个轮到去休息的人就坐在舵杠

旁边。我们看出海湾里那朵红光，向它驶去，猜它一定指出某一个泊船的小港。我们驶过两只船，异乡情调的，船尾很高的，抛锚睡着；当我们走近那现在是很朦胧的红光，我们小艇的船头碰到一只突出码头的末端。我们疲倦得瞎了眼睛了。我的水手放松船桨，从坐板上摔下，仿佛死了。我把船系在一根大桩上。一阵湖流轻轻地潺潺着。岸上芬芳的黑暗集成庞大的一堆一堆，那是密生的大丛植物，也许是——寂然的，古怪的东西。在它们脚下，半圆形的海滨微微闪光，像一番幻梦。绝无灯光，绝无动弹，绝无声响。神秘的东方对着我，它是香得像一朵花，静得同死一样，暗得同坟一样。

"我是坐着，疲倦得不能以文字形容，狂欢有如一个战胜者，睡不着，神魂颠倒，好像当前有一个深奥的，命运攸关的谜。

"桨溅水的声音，水面回响的有规律的打水声，跟岸的寂静相比变为大声的拍打，使我跳起来。一只小艇，一只欧洲的小艇，驶进来。我呼唤已死者的名字；我喊：'犹太！'一个细邈的喊声回答。

"这是船主。我比主艇先到三点钟；我很高兴，再听到老头子颤动的，疲累的声音：'是你吗，马罗？''当心码头的末端，先生，'我喊。

"他小心地走近，用深海的铅线把船弄靠岸，这些线把我们救出来——为着保险商。我放宽我的船缆，落到同它一排。他坐在船尾，一个精神涣散的人，沾着露水，他的双手叉在怀中。他的水手都已睡着了。'我受了许多辛苦困难，'他低声说。'马洪在后面——没有隔多远。'我们说话是用耳语，低声的耳语，好像只怕扰醒这片大陆。至于水手，那时炮声、雷声、地震都不能把他们弄醒。

"我们谈时，向四面望，我看见一盏明灯在夜的海里航行。'那里有一只汽船走过海湾，'我说。它不是过路，它是进口，它甚至于走近泊下。'我希望，'老头子说，'你去打听它是否是英国船。也许他们能够带我们到别地方去。'他好像焦急得神经很受震动。于是靠着拧同踢，我把我的一个水手弄到睡游的状态，给他一个桨，自己另拿一把，向汽船的灯光划去。

"船上有喋喋的说话声，机器房金属家伙空

洞的铿锵声，甲板上的脚步声。它的舷侧门发光，圆得像睁大的眼睛。人影在船上走动，有一个模糊人形高高地站在舰桥上。他听到我的划桨声音。

"然后，在我能够开口之前，东方向我说话，但是用的是西方的口腔。一大阵的话倾注到谜一般的，命运也似的静默里去；异乡情调的怒语，杂有几个字，甚至于整句的发音清晰的英文，这虽然没有那么异乡的，可是更令人惊奇。这个人拼命地赌咒发誓；用一串连珠的毁骂使海湾严重的静默变成莫名其妙。起先叫我做猪，于是步步上升，说出不能出口的形容字——用英文说。站在上面的人用两种语言大声怒骂，气得那么真挚样子，几乎使我相信我有些冒犯了大宇宙的和谐。我差不多看不见他，但是开始想他将气得晕倒了。

"忽然间他停住，我能听到他鼻孔喷气同喘息像一只海豚。

"我说：'这是什么汽船？'

"'哎？怎么样？你是谁？'

"'一只在海上着火的英国帆船的飘零水手。

我们今晚来到这里。我是二副。船主在长艇里，想知道你肯不肯带我们到别的地方去。'

"'啊，我的天呀！我说……这是'天国'从新加坡回去。早上我将同你船主商量……还有……我说……你刚才听见我说话没有？'

"'我想海湾里所有的人们都听到你的话了。'

"'我以为你是一只本地的船。现在，你看——这个该死的懒流氓，这个看守者又去睡了——真是该咒。灯光又灭了，我几乎撞着这可恶的码头。这是第三次他跟我开这玩笑。现在我问你，有谁能够忍受这种事情吗？这足够叫人气疯了。我要把他报告上去。……我要使驻外外交副代表把他开除，我敢赌……！你看——那里并没有亮。已经灭了，是不是？我要你做见证，那个亮是灭了。那里应当有个亮，你知道。一盏红灯在……'

"'那里起先有个亮，'我温和地说。

"'但是它灭了，汉子！这样谈论有什么用呢？你自己能够看见它是灭了——你看得见吗？若使你领一艘宝贵的汽船，走过这个上帝所弃的海岸，你也会要一盏灯。我将把这流氓从他这可

怜的码头这一头踢到那上头。你看我会不会放松
他。我一定——'

"'那么我可以告诉我的船主你肯带我们走？'
我打断他的话。

"'是的，我将带你们一同走。再见，'他粗
鲁地说道。

"我划回去，又把船缚在码头旁边，于是最
后去睡觉。我会面对东方的静默了，我会听到它
的一些语言了。但是当我再睁开眼睛，它的静默
是这么完整，仿佛从来没有破坏过。我是躺在大
光明底下，天空从来没有像这么辽远，这么高
朗。我睁开眼睛，毫不动弹地躺着。

"然后我看见东方的人们——他们望着我。
码头上满是人。我看棕色的，青铜色的，黄色的
脸孔，黑眼睛，一队东方群众的灿烂夺目，色调
辉煌。这班人眼睛盯着我们，没有一点说话的声
音，没有一声的叹息，没有丝毫的转动。他们直
着眼睛看下面的小船艇，看夜里从海外来到他们
这儿这几个睡着的人们。一切东西都是静的。棕
树的叶子安详地站着，天空衬在后面。沿岸的树
林没有一枝摇动，隐着瞧不见的屋子的棕色屋顶

偷偷地现在绿荫之中，现在发光挂着，静止得有
如重铁铸成的大叶子之中。这是古代航海家的东
方，这么古老，这么神秘，灿烂而忧郁，虽然生
气勃勃，却永远不变，满是危险同希望。这班就
是东方的人们。我忽然坐起来。群众里有一个波
动从这头一直达到那头，大家的头都向一边倾，
大家的身体都这么摆动，这个激动像水面的波
纹，田中的微风——一下子大家又归于静止。想
起来如在目前——一大片的海湾，闪烁的沙滩，
庞杂的，无限的绿色世界，蓝得像梦里海洋的大
海，一群注视的脸孔，鲜艳颜色的衣服跟火焰一
般——这些全被水反映出来，还有一弯的海岸，
码头，恬静地浮在水面的船尾很高的异乡船只，
带着从西方来睡着的疲劳的人们的三条小船，这
几个人完全不觉得这个国土，这里人民同太阳的
猛烈。他们熟睡，有的横躺在坐板上面，有的蜷
伏在船底板子上面，那种不在乎的态度简直同死
一样。肯倚着长艇船尾的船主的头垂到他的胸
际，看起来他好像永不会醒来。再远一些，马洪
脸朝着天，白色的长须摊在他胸前，好像他坐舵
扛旁被人枪射了；还有一个人，弯成一团在船

首，睡时双臂抱着龙骨，他的脸颊放在船沿。东方没有声音地望着他们。

"此后我知道了它的魔力；看见了神秘的海岸，静止的水，棕色人种的国土，那里有一个阴险的'报复之神'埋伏着，追赶，袭击这许多来征服的种族，这些种族却自夸他们的聪明，他们的知识，他们的力气。但是对于我，整个东方是包括在我年青时这一瞥眼。这完全是在我向他睁开我年少眼睛的那一刹那。我从同海恶斗一场来到它这里——我正年青——我看它望着我。这就是它所留下的唯一印象！只一刹那；具有魅力，浪漫性，魔力——青春的一刹那？……阳光突然射到异乡的海岸，值得记忆的时候，引起一声长叹的时候，于是就是——再见！——毁灭后的沉沉黑夜——永诀……！"

他喝酒。

"啊！从前良好的时光——从前良好的时光。青春同海。魔力同海！良好的，有力的大海，咸味的，刻毒的大海，它能够向你细语，向你咆哮，把你打得没有气。"

他喝酒。

　　"最奇怪却是海，我相信，是海——或者是青春？谁知道？但是你们诸位——你们从人生都得到一些东西：金钱，爱情——无论你在岸上得到了什么东西——请告诉我，那是不是绝妙的时光，当我们年青在海上漂游；年青，什么东西都没有，在海上，那是什么东西都不给的，除开猛烈的打击——有时给你们一个感到自己力气的机会——唯有这个——是你们所不能忘怀的吗？"

　　我们都向他颔首：理财家，会计员，律师，我们都向他颔首，对着这明亮的桌子，它像一片棕色的止水反映出我们画有线的，满是皱纹的脸孔；我们被劳工，欺骗，成功，爱情加上标志的脸孔；我们疲倦的眼睛还是，永远是，焦急地想从人生里得到某件东西，那当我们期望的时候，已经逃掉了——不知不觉之间消灭了，一声叹息，一下闪光之间没有了——连同青春，魅力，同幻境的浪漫情调。

YOUTH

*T*his could have occurred nowhere but in England, where men and sea interpenetrate, so to speak—the sea entering into the life of most men, and the men knowing something or everything about the sea, in the way of amusement, of travel, or of bread-winning.

We were sitting round a mahogany table that reflected the bottle, the claret-glasses, and our faces as we leaned on our elbows. There was a director of companies, an accountant, a lawyer, Marlow, and myself. The director had been a Conway boy, the accountant had served four years at sea, the lawyer—a fine crusted Tory, High Churchman, the best of old fellows, the soul of honour—had been chief officer in the P. & O. service in the good old days when mail-boats were square-rigged at least on two masts, and used to come down the China Sea before a fair monsoon with stun'-sails set alow and aloft. We all began life in the merchant service. Between the five of us there was the strong bond of the sea, and also the fellowship of the craft, which no amount of enthusiasm for yachting, cruising, and so on can give, since one is only the amusement of life and the other is life itself.

Marlow (at least I think that is how he spelt his name) told the story, or rather the chronicle, of a voyage.

"Yes, I have seen a little of the Eastern seas; but what I remember best is my first voyage there. You fellows know there are those voyages that seem ordered for the illustration of life that might stand for a symbol of existence. You fight, work, sweat, nearly kill yourself, sometimes do kill yourself, trying to accomplish something—and you can't. Not from any fault of yours. You simply can do nothing, neither great nor little—not a thing in the world—not even marry an old maid, or get a wretched 600-ton cargo of coal to its port of destination.

"It was altogether a memorable affair. It was my first voyage to the East, and my first voyage as second mate; it was also my skipper's first command. You'll admit it was time. He was sixty if a day; a little man, with a broad, not very straight back, with bowed shoulders and one leg more bandy than the other, he had that queer twisted-about appearance you see so often in men who work in the fields. He had a nut-cracker face—chin and nose trying to come together over a sunken mouth—and it was framed in iron-grey fluffy hair, that looked like a chin strap of cotton-wool sprinkled with coal-dust. And he had blue eyes in that old face of his, which were amazingly like a boy's, with that candid expression some quite common men preserve to the end of their days by a rare internal gift of simplicity of heart and rectitude of soul. What induced him to accept me was a wonder. I had come out of a crack Australian clipper, where I had been third officer, and he seemed to have a prejudice against crack clippers as aristocratic and high-toned. He said to me, 'You know, in this ship you will have to work.' I said I had to work in every ship I had ever been in. 'Ah, but this is different, and you gentlemen out of them big ships... but there! I dare say you will do. Join to-morrow.'

"I joined to-morrow. It was twenty-two years ago; and I was just twenty. How time passes! It was one of the happiest days of my life. Fancy! Second mate for the first time—a really responsible officer! I wouldn't have thrown up my new billet for a fortune. The mate looked me over carefully. He was also an old chap, but of another stamp. He had a Roman nose, a snow-white, long beard, and his name was Mahon, but he insisted that it should be pronounced Mann. He was well connected; yet there was something wrong with his luck, and he had never got on.

"As to the captain, he had been for years in coasters, then in the Mediterranean, and last in the West Indian trade. He had never been round the Capes. He could just write a kind of sketchy hand, and didn't care for writing at all. Both were thorough good seamen of course, and between those two old chaps I felt like a small boy between two grandfathers.

"The ship also was old. Her name was the Judea. Queer name, isn't it? She belonged to a man Wilmer, Wilcox—some name like that; but he has been bankrupt and dead these twenty years or more, and his name doesn't matter. She had been laid up in Shadwell basin for ever so long. You may imagine her state. She was all rust, dust, grime— soot aloft, dirt on deck. To me it was like coming out of a palace into a ruined cottage. She was about 400 tons, had a primitive windlass, wooden latches to the doors, not a bit of brass about her, and a big square stern. There was on it, below her name in big letters, a lot of scroll work, with the gilt off, and some sort of a coat of arms, with the motto 'Do or Die' underneath. I remember it took my fancy immensely. There was a touch of romance in it, something that made me love the old thing—something that appealed to my youth!

"We left London in ballast—sand ballast—to load a cargo of coal in a northern port for Bangkok. Bangkok! I thrilled. I had been six years at sea, but had only seen Melbourne and Sydney, very good places, charming places in their way—but Bangkok!

"We worked out of the Thames under canvas, with a North Sea pilot on board. His name was Jermyn, and he dodged all day long about the galley drying his handkerchief before the stove. Apparently he never slept. He was a dismal man, with a perpetual tear sparkling at the end of his nose, who either had been in trouble, or was in trouble, or expected to be in trouble—couldn't be happy unless something went wrong. He mistrusted my youth, my common-sense, and my seamanship, and made a point of showing it in a hundred little ways. I dare say he was right. It seems to me I knew very little then, and I know not much more now; but I cherish a hate for that Jermyn to this day.

"We were a week working up as far as Yarmouth Roads, and then we got into a gale—the famous October gale of twenty-two years ago. It was wind, lightning, sleet, snow, and a terrific sea. We were flying light, and you may imagine how bad it was when I tell you we had smashed bulwarks and a flooded deck. On the second night she shifted her ballast into the lee bow, and by that time we had been blown off somewhere on the Dogger Bank. There was nothing for it but go below with shovels and try to right her, and there we were in that vast hold, gloomy like a cavern, the tallow dips stuck and flickering on the beams, the gale howling above, the ship tossing about like mad on her side; there we all were, Jermyn, the captain, everyone, hardly able to keep our feet, engaged on that gravedigger's work, and trying to toss shovelfuls of wet sand up to windward. At every tumble of the ship you could see vaguely in the dim light men falling down with a great flourish of shovels. One of the ship's boys (we had two), impressed by the weirdness of the scene, wept as if his heart would break. We could hear him blubbering somewhere in the shadows.

"On the third day the gale died out, and by-and-by a north-country tug picked us up. We took sixteen days in all to get from London to the Tyne! When we got into dock we had lost our turn for loading, and they hauled us off to a tier where we remained for a month. Mrs. Beard (the captain's name was Beard) came from Colchester to see the old man. She lived on board. The crew of runners had left, and there remained only the officers, one boy, and the steward, a mulatto who answered to the name of Abraham. Mrs. Beard was an old woman, with a face all wrinkled and ruddy like a winter apple, and the figure of a young girl. She caught sight of me once, sewing on a button, and insisted on having my shirts to repair. This was something different from the captains' wives I had known on board crack clippers. When I brought her the shirts, she said, 'And the socks? They want mending, I am sure, and John's—Captain Beard's—things are all in order now. I would be glad of something to do.' Bless the old woman! She overhauled my outfit for me, and meantime I read for the first time Sartor Resartus and Burnaby's Ride to Khiva. I didn't understand much of the first then; but I remember I preferred the soldier to the philosopher at the time; a preference which life has only confirmed. One was a man, and the other was either more—or less. However, they are both dead, and Mrs. Beard is dead, and youth, strength, genius, thoughts, achievements, simple hearts—all dies ... No matter.

"They loaded us at last. We shipped a crew, eight able seamen and two boys. We hauled off one evening to the buoys at the dock-gates, ready to go out, and with a fair prospect of beginning the voyage next day. Mrs. Beard was to start for home by a late train. When the ship was fast we went to tea. We sat rather silent through the meal—Mahon, the old couple, and I. I finished first, and slipped away for a smoke, my cabin being in a deck-house just against the poop. It was high water, blowing fresh with a drizzle; the double dock-gates were opened, and the steam colliers were going in and out in the darkness with their lights burning bright, a great plashing of propellers, rattling of winches, and a lot of hailing on the pier-heads. I watched the procession of head-lights gliding high and of green lights gliding low in the night, when suddenly a red gleam flashed at me, vanished, came into view again, and remained. The fore-end of a steamer loomed up close. I shouted down the cabin, 'Come up, quick!' and then heard a startled voice saying afar in the dark, 'Stop her, sir.' A bell jingled. Another voice cried warningly, 'We are going right into that barque, sir.' The answer to this was a gruff 'All right,' and the next thing was a heavy crash as the steamer struck a glancing blow with the bluff of her bow about our fore-rigging. There was a moment of confusion, yelling, and running about. Steam roared. Then somebody was heard saying, 'All clear, sir.'... 'Are you all right?' asked the gruff voice. I had jumped forward to see the damage, and hailed back, 'I think so.' 'Easy

astern,' said the gruff voice. A bell jingled. 'What
steamer is that?' screamed Mahon. By that time she
was no more to us than a bulky shadow maneuvering
a little way off. They shouted at us some name—a
woman's name, Miranda or Melissa—or some such
thing. 'This means another month in this beastly
hole,' said Mahon to me, as we peered with lamps
about the splintered bulwarks and broken braces. 'But
where's the captain?'

"We had not heard or seen anything of him
all that time. We went aft to look. A doleful voice
arose hailing somewhere in the middle of the dock,
'Judea ahoy!'... How the devil did he get there? ...
'Hallo!' we shouted. 'I am adrift in our boat without
oars,' he cried. A belated waterman offered his
services, and Mahon struck a bargain with him for
half-a-crown to tow our skipper alongside; but it was
Mrs. Beard that came up the ladder first. They had
been floating about the dock in that mizzly cold rain
for nearly an hour. I was never so surprised in my
life.

"It appears that when he heard my shout 'Come up,' he understood at once what was the matter, caught up his wife, ran on deck, and across, and down into our boat, which was fast to the ladder. Not bad for a sixty-year-old. Just imagine that old fellow saving heroically in his arms that old woman—the woman of his life. He set her down on a thwart, and was ready to climb back on board when the painter came adrift somehow, and away they went together. Of course in the confusion we did not hear him shouting. He looked abashed. She said cheerfully, 'I suppose it does not matter my losing the train now?' 'No, Jenny—you go below and get warm,' he growled. Then to us, 'A sailor has no business with a wife—I say. There I was, out of the ship. Well, no harm done this time. Let's go and look at what that fool of a steamer smashed.'

"It wasn't much, but it delayed us three weeks. At the end of that time, the captain being engaged with his agents, I carried Mrs. Beard's bag to the railway-station and put her all comfy into a third-class carriage. She lowered the window to say, 'You are a good young man. If you see John—Captain Beard—without his muffler at night, just remind him from me to keep his throat well wrapped up.' 'Certainly, Mrs. Beard,' I said. 'You are a good young man; I noticed how attentive you are to John—to Captain—' The train pulled out suddenly; I took my cap off to the old woman: I never saw her again... Pass the bottle.

"We went to sea next day. When we made that start for Bangkok we had been already three months out of London. We had expected to be a fortnight or so—at the outside.

"It was January, and the weather was beautiful—the beautiful sunny winter weather that has more charm than in the summer-time, because it is unexpected, and crisp, and you know it won't, it can't, last long. It's like a windfall, like a godsend, like an unexpected piece of luck.

"It lasted all down the North Sea, all down Channel; and it lasted till we were three hundred miles or so to the westward of the Lizards: then the wind went round to the sou'west and began to pipe up. In two days it blew a gale. The Judea, hove to, wallowed on the Atlantic like an old candle box. It blew day after day: it blew with spite, without interval, without mercy, without rest. The world was nothing but an immensity of great foaming waves rushing at us, under a sky low enough to touch with the hand and dirty like a smoked ceiling. In the stormy space surrounding us there was as much flying spray as air. Day after day and night after night there was nothing round the ship but the howl of the wind, the tumult of the sea, the noise of water pouring over her deck. There was no rest for her and no rest for us. She tossed, she pitched, she stood on her head, she sat on her tail, she rolled, she groaned, and we had to hold on while on deck and cling to our bunks when below, in a constant effort of body and worry of mind.

"One night Mahon spoke through the small window of my berth. It opened right into my very bed, and I was lying there sleepless, in my boots, feeling as though I had not slept for years, and could not if I tried. He said excitedly—

"'You got the sounding-rod in here, Marlow? I can't get the pumps to suck. By God! It's no child's play.'

"I gave him the sounding-rod and lay down again, trying to think of various things—but I thought only of the pumps. When I came on deck they were still at it, and my watch relieved at the pumps. By the light of the lantern brought on deck to examine the sounding-rod, I caught a glimpse of their weary, serious faces. We pumped all the four hours. We pumped all night, all day, all the week,— watch and watch. She was working herself loose, and leaked badly—not enough to drown us at once, but enough to kill us with the work at the pumps. And while we pumped the ship was going from us piecemeal: the bulwarks went, the stanchions were torn out, the ventilators smashed, the cabin-door burst in. There was not a dry spot in the ship. She was being gutted bit by bit. The long-boat changed, as if by magic, into matchwood where she stood in her gripes. I had lashed her myself, and was rather proud of my handiwork, which had withstood so long the malice of the sea. And we pumped. And there was no break in the weather. The sea was white like a sheet of foam, like a caldron of boiling milk; there was not a break in the clouds, no—not the size of a man's hand—no, not for so much as ten seconds. There was for us no sky, there were for us no stars, no sun, no universe—nothing but angry clouds and an infuriated sea. We pumped watch and watch, for dear life; and it seemed to last for months, for years, for all eternity, as though we had been dead and gone to a hell for sailors. We forgot the day of the week, the name of the month, what year it was, and whether we had ever been ashore. The sails blew away, she lay broadside on under a weather-cloth, the ocean poured over her, and we did not care. We turned those handles, and had the eyes of idiots. As soon as we had crawled on deck

I used to take a round turn with a rope about the men, the pumps, and the mainmast, and we turned, we turned incessantly, with the water to our waists, to our necks, over our heads. It was all one. We had forgotten how it felt to be dry.

"And there was somewhere in me the thought: By Jove! This is the deuce of an adventure— something you read about; and it is my first voyage as second mate—and I am only twenty—and here I am lasting it out as well as any of these men, and keeping my chaps up to the mark. I was pleased. I would not have given up the experience for worlds. I had moments of exultation. Whenever the old dismantled craft pitched heavily with her counter high in the air, she seemed to me to throw up, like an appeal, like a defiance, like a cry to the clouds without mercy, the words written on her stern, 'Judea, London. Do or Die.'

"O youth! The strength of it, the faith of it, the imagination of it! To me she was not an old rattle-trap carting about the world a lot of coal for a freight—to me she was the endeavor, the test, the trial of life. I think of her with pleasure, with affection, with regret—as you would think of someone dead you have loved. I shall never forget her.... Pass the bottle.

"One night when tied to the mast, as I explained, we were pumping on, deafened with the wind, and without spirit enough in us to wish ourselves dead, a heavy sea crashed aboard and swept clean over us. As soon as I got my breath I shouted, as in duty bound, 'Keep on, boys!' When suddenly I felt something hard floating on deck strike the calf of my leg. I made a grab at it and missed. It was so dark we could not see each other's faces within a foot—you understand.

"After that thump the ship kept quiet for a while, and the thing, whatever it was, struck my leg again. This time I caught it—and it was a saucepan. At first, being stupid with fatigue and thinking of nothing but the pumps, I did not understand what I had in my hand. Suddenly it dawned upon me, and

I shouted, 'Boys, the house on deck is gone. Leave this, and let's look for the cook.'

"There was a deck-house forward, which contained the galley, the cook's berth, and the quarters of the crew. As we had expected for days to see it swept away, the hands had been ordered to sleep in the cabin—the only safe place in the ship. The steward, Abraham, however, persisted in clinging to his berth, stupidly, like a mule— from sheer fright I believe, like an animal that won't leave a stable falling in an earthquake. So we went to look for him. It was chancing death, since once out of our lashings we were as exposed as if on a raft. But we went. The house was shattered as if a shell had exploded inside. Most of it had gone overboard—stove, men's quarters, and their property, all was gone; but two posts, holding a portion of the bulkhead to which Abraham's bunk was attached, remained as if by a miracle. We groped in the ruins and came upon this, and there he was, sitting in his bunk, surrounded by foam and wreckage, jabbering cheerfully to himself. He was out of his mind; completely and for ever mad, with this sudden shock coming upon the fag-end of his endurance. We snatched him up, lugged him aft, and pitched him head-first down the cabin companion. You understand there was no time to carry him down with infinite precautions and wait to see how he got on. Those below would pick him up at the bottom of the stairs all right. We were in a hurry to go back to the pumps. That business could not wait. A bad leak is an inhuman thing.

"One would think that the sole purpose of that fiendish gale had been to make a lunatic of that poor devil of a mulatto. It eased before morning, and next day the sky cleared, and as the sea went down the leak took up. When it came to bending a fresh set of sails the crew demanded to put back—and really there was nothing else to do. Boats gone, decks swept clean, cabin gutted, men without a stitch but what they stood in, stores spoiled, ship strained. We put her head for home, and—would you believe it?

The wind came east right in our teeth. It blew fresh, it blew continuously. We had to beat up every inch of the way, but she did not leak so badly, the water keeping comparatively smooth. Two hours' pumping in every four is no joke—but it kept her afloat as far as Falmouth.

"The good people there live on casualties of the sea, and no doubt were glad to see us. A hungry crowd of shipwrights sharpened their chisels at the sight of that carcass of a ship. And, by Jove! They had pretty pickings off us before they were done. I fancy the owner was already in a tight place. There were delays. Then it was decided to take part of the cargo out and calk her topsides. This was done, the repairs finished, cargo re-shipped; a new crew came on board, and we went out—for Bangkok. At the end of a week we were back again. The crew said they weren't going to Bangkok—a hundred and fifty days' passage—in a something hooker that wanted pumping eight hours out of the twenty-four; and the nautical papers inserted again the little paragraph, ' Judea. Barque. Tyne to Bangkok; coals; put back to Falmouth leaky and with crew refusing duty.'

"There were more delays—more tinkering. The owner came down for a day, and said she was as right as a little fiddle. Poor old Captain Beard looked like the ghost of a Geordie skipper—through the worry and humiliation of it. Remember he was sixty, and it was his first command. Mahon said it was a foolish business, and would end badly. I loved the ship more than ever, and wanted awfully to get to Bangkok. To Bangkok! Magic name, blessed name. Mesopotamia wasn't a patch on it. Remember I was twenty, and it was my first second mate's billet, and the East was waiting for me.

"We went out and anchored in the outer roads with a fresh crew—the third. She leaked worse than ever. It was as if those confounded shipwrights had actually made a hole in her. This time we did not even go outside. The crew simply refused to man the windlass.

"They towed us back to the inner harbour, and we became a fixture, a feature, an institution of the place. People pointed us out to visitors as 'That 'ere bark that's going to Bangkok—has been here six months—put back three times.' On holidays the small boys pulling about in boats would hail, 'Judea, ahoy!' and if a head showed above the rail shouted, 'Where you bound to?—Bangkok?' and jeered. We were only three on board. The poor old skipper mooned in the cabin. Mahon undertook the cooking, and unexpectedly developed all a Frenchman's genius for preparing nice little messes. I looked languidly after the rigging. We became citizens of Falmouth. Every shopkeeper knew us. At the barber's or tobacconist's they asked familiarly, 'Do you think you will ever get to Bangkok?' Meantime the owner, the underwriters, and the charterers squabbled amongst themselves in London, and our pay went on.... Pass the bottle.

"It was horrid. Morally it was worse than pumping for life. It seemed as though we had been forgotten by the world, belonged to nobody, would get nowhere; it seemed that, as if bewitched, we would have to live for ever and ever in that inner harbour, a derision and a by-word to generations of long-shore loafers and dishonest boatmen. I obtained three months' pay and a five days' leave, and made a rush for London. It took me a day to get there and pretty well another to come back—but three months' pay went all the same. I don't know what I did with it. I went to a music-hall, I believe, lunched, dined, and supped in a swell place in Regent Street, and was back to time, with nothing but a complete set of Byron's works and a new railway rug to show for three months' work. The boatman who pulled me off to the ship said, 'Hallo! I thought you had left the old thing. She will never get to Bangkok.' 'That's all you know about it,' I said scornfully—but I didn't like that prophecy at all.

"Suddenly a man, some kind of agent to somebody, appeared with full powers. He had grog-blossoms all over his face, an indomitable energy, and was a jolly soul. We leaped into life again. A hulk came alongside, took our cargo, and then we went into dry dock to get our copper stripped. No wonder she leaked. The poor thing, strained beyond endurance by the gale, had, as if in disgust, spat out all the oakum of her lower seams. She was recalked, new coppered, and made as tight as a bottle. We went back to the hulk and re-shipped our cargo.

"Then on a fine moonlight night, all the rats left the ship.

"We had been infested with them. They had destroyed our sails, consumed more stores than the crew, affably shared our beds and our dangers, and now, when the ship was made seaworthy, concluded to clear out. I called Mahon to enjoy the spectacle. Rat after rat appeared on our rail, took a last look over his shoulder, and leaped with a hollow thud into the empty hulk. We tried to count them, but soon lost the tale. Mahon said, 'Well, well! Don't talk to me about the intelligence of rats. They ought to have left before, when we had that narrow squeak from foundering. There you have the proof how silly is the superstition about them. They leave a good ship for an old rotten hulk, where there is nothing to eat, too, the fools! ... I don't believe they know what is safe or what is good for them, any more than you or I.'

"And after some more talk we agreed that the wisdom of rats had been grossly overrated, being in fact no greater than that of men.

"The story of the ship was known, by this, all up the Channel from Land's End to the Forelands, and we could get no crew on the south coast. They sent us one all complete from Liverpool, and we left once more—for Bangkok.

"We had fair breezes, smooth water right into the tropics, and the old Judea lumbered along in the sunshine. When she went eight knots everything cracked aloft, and we tied our caps to our heads; but mostly she strolled on at the rate of three miles an hour. What could you expect? She was tired—that old ship. Her youth was where mine is—where yours is—you fellows who listen to this yarn; and what friend would throw your years and your weariness in your face? We didn't grumble at her. To us aft, at least, it seemed as though we had been born in her, reared in her, had lived in her for ages, had never known any other ship. I would just as soon have abused the old village church at home for not being a cathedral.

"And for me there was also my youth to make me patient. There was all the East before me, and all life, and the thought that I had been tried in that ship and had come out pretty well. And I thought of men of old who, centuries ago, went that road in ships that sailed no better, to the land of palms, and spices, and yellow sands, and of brown nations ruled by kings more cruel than Nero the Roman and more splendid than Solomon the Jew. The old bark lumbered on, heavy with her age and the burden of her cargo, while I lived the life of youth in ignorance and hope. She lumbered on through an interminable procession of days; and the fresh gilding flashed back at the setting sun, seemed to cry out over the darkening sea the words painted on her stern, 'Judea, London. Do or Die.'

"Then we entered the Indian Ocean and steered northerly for Java Head. The winds were light. Weeks slipped by. She crawled on, do or die, and people at home began to think of posting us as overdue.

"One Saturday evening, I being off duty, the men asked me to give them an extra bucket of water or so—for washing clothes. As I did not wish to screw on the fresh-water pump so late, I went forward whistling, and with a key in my hand to unlock the forepeak scuttle, intending to serve the water out of a spare tank we kept there.

"The smell down below was as unexpected as it was frightful. One would have thought hundreds of paraffin-lamps had been flaring and smoking in that hole for days. I was glad to get out. The man with me coughed and said, 'Funny smell, sir.' I answered negligently, 'It's good for the health, they say,' and walked aft.

"The first thing I did was to put my head down the square of the midship ventilator. As I lifted the lid a visible breath, something like a thin fog, a puff of faint haze, rose from the opening. The ascending air was hot, and had a heavy, sooty, paraffinic smell. I gave one sniff, and put down the lid gently. It was no use choking myself. The cargo was on fire.

"Next day she began to smoke in earnest. You see it was to be expected, for though the coal was of a safe kind, that cargo had been so handled, so broken up with handling that it looked more like smithy coal than anything else. Then it had been wetted—more than once. It rained all the time we were taking it back from the hulk, and now with this long passage it got heated, and there was another case of spontaneous combustion.

"The captain called us into the cabin. He had a chart spread on the table, and looked unhappy. He said, 'The coast of West Australia is near, but I mean to proceed to our destination. It is the hurricane month too; but we will just keep her head for

Bangkok, and fight the fire. No more putting back anywhere, if we all get roasted. We will try first to stifle this 'ere damned combustion by want of air.'

"We tried. We battened down everything, and still she smoked. The smoke kept coming out through imperceptible crevices; it forced itself through bulkheads and covers; it oozed here and there and everywhere in slender threads, in an invisible film, in an incomprehensible manner. It made its way into the cabin, into the forecastle; it poisoned the sheltered places on the deck, it could be sniffed as high as the main-yard. It was clear that if the smoke came out the air came in. This was disheartening. This combustion refused to be stifled.

"We resolved to try water, and took the hatches off. Enormous volumes of smoke, whitish, yellowish, thick, greasy, misty, choking, ascended as high as the trucks. All hands cleared out aft. Then the poisonous cloud blew away, and we went back to work in a smoke that was no thicker now than that of an ordinary factory chimney.

"We rigged the force pump, got the hose along, and by-and-by it burst. Well, it was as old as the ship—a prehistoric hose, and past repair. Then we pumped with the feeble head-pump, drew water with buckets, and in this way managed in time to pour lots of Indian Ocean into the main hatch. The bright stream flashed in sunshine, fell into a layer of white crawling smoke, and vanished on the black surface of coal. Steam ascended mingling with the smoke. We poured salt water as into a barrel without a bottom. It was our fate to pump in that ship, to pump out of her, to pump into her; and after keeping water out of her to save ourselves from being drowned, we frantically poured water into her to save ourselves from being burnt.

"And she crawled on, do or die, in the serene weather. The sky was a miracle of purity, a miracle of azure. The sea was polished, was blue, was pellucid, was sparkling like a precious stone, extending on all sides, all round to the horizon — as if the whole terrestrial globe had been one jewel, one colossal sapphire, a single gem fashioned into a planet. And on the luster of the great calm waters the Judea glided imperceptibly, enveloped in languid and unclean vapours, in a lazy cloud that drifted to leeward, light and slow: a pestiferous cloud defiling the splendour of sea and sky.

"All this time of course we saw no fire. The cargo smoldered at the bottom somewhere. Once Mahon, as we were working side by side, said to me with a queer smile, 'Now, if she only would spring a tidy leak—like that time when we first left the Channel—it would put a stopper on this fire. Wouldn't it?' I remarked irrelevantly, 'Do you remember the rats?'

"We fought the fire and sailed the ship too as carefully as though nothing had been the matter. The steward cooked and attended on us. Of the other twelve men, eight worked while four rested. Everyone took his turn, captain included. There was equality, and if not exactly fraternity, then a deal of good feeling. Sometimes a man, as he dashed a bucketful of water down the hatchway, would yell out, 'Hurrah for Bangkok!' and the rest laughed. But generally we were taciturn and serious—and thirsty. Oh! How thirsty! And we had to be careful with the water. Strict allowance. The ship smoked, the sun blazed... Pass the bottle.

"We tried everything. We even made an attempt to dig down to the fire. No good, of course. No man could remain more than a minute below. Mahon, who went first, fainted there, and the man who went to fetch him out did likewise. We lugged them out on deck. Then I leaped down to show how easily it could be done. They had learned wisdom by that time, and contented themselves by fishing for me with a chain-hook tied to a broom-handle, I believe. I did not offer to go and fetch up my shovel, which was left down below.

"Things began to look bad. We put the long-boat into the water. The second boat was ready to swing out. We had also another, a fourteen-foot thing, on davits aft, where it was quite safe.

"Then behold, the smoke suddenly decreased. We re-doubled our efforts to flood the bottom of the ship. In two days there was no smoke at all. Everybody was on the broad grin. This was on a Friday. On Saturday no work, but sailing the ship of course was done. The men washed their clothes and their faces for the first time in a fortnight, and had a special dinner given them. They spoke of spontaneous combustion with contempt, and implied they were the boys to put out combustions. Somehow we all felt as though we each had inherited a large fortune. But a beastly smell of burning hung about the ship. Captain Beard had hollow eyes and sunken cheeks. I had never noticed so much before how twisted and bowed he was. He and Mahon prowled soberly about hatches and ventilators, sniffing. It struck me suddenly poor Mahon was a very, very old chap. As to me, I was as pleased and proud as though I had helped to win a great naval battle. O! Youth!

"The night was fine. In the morning a

homeward-bound ship passed us hull down,—the first we had seen for months; but we were nearing the land at last, Java Head being about 190 miles off, and nearly due north.

"Next day it was my watch on deck from eight to twelve. At breakfast the captain observed, 'It's wonderful how that smell hangs about the cabin.' About ten, the mate being on the poop, I stepped down on the main-deck for a moment. The carpenter's bench stood abaft the mainmast: I leaned against it sucking at my pipe, and the carpenter, a young chap, came to talk to me. He remarked, 'I think we have done very well, haven't we?' and then I perceived with annoyance the fool was trying to tilt the bench. I said curtly, 'Don't, Chips,' and immediately became aware of a queer sensation, of an absurd delusion,—I seemed somehow to be in the air. I heard all round me like a pent-up breath released—as if a thousand giants simultaneously had said Phoo!—and felt a dull concussion which made my ribs ache suddenly. No doubt about it—

I was in the air, and my body was describing a short parabola. But short as it was, I had the time to think several thoughts in, as far as I can remember, the following order, 'This can't be the carpenter—What is it?—Some accident—Submarine volcano?—Coals, gas!—By Jove! We are being blown up—Everybody's dead—I am falling into the after-hatch—I see fire in it.'

"The coal-dust suspended in the air of the hold had glowed dull-red at the moment of the explosion. In the twinkling of an eye, in an infinitesimal fraction of a second since the first tilt of the bench, I was sprawling full length on the cargo. I picked myself up and scrambled out. It was quick like a rebound. The deck was a wilderness of smashed timber, lying crosswise like trees in a wood after a hurricane; an immense curtain of soiled rags waved gently before me—it was the mainsail blown to strips. I thought, the masts will be toppling over directly; and to get out of the way bolted on all-fours towards the poop-ladder. The first person I saw was Mahon, with eyes like saucers, his mouth open, and the long white hair standing straight on end round his head like a silver halo. He was just about to go down when the sight of the main-deck stirring, heaving up, and changing into splinters before his eyes, petrified him on the top step. I stared at him in unbelief, and he stared at me with a queer kind of shocked curiosity. I did not know that I had no hair, no eyebrows, no eyelashes; that my young moustache was burnt off; that my face was black, one cheek laid open, my nose cut, and my chin bleeding. I had lost my cap, one of my slippers, and my shirt was torn to rags. Of all this I was not aware. I was amazed to see the ship still afloat, the poop-deck whole—and, most of all, to see anybody alive. Also the peace of the sky and the serenity of the sea were distinctly surprising. I suppose I expected to see them convulsed with horror... Pass the bottle.

"There was a voice hailing the ship from somewhere—in the air, in the sky—I couldn't tell. Presently I saw the captain—and he was mad. He asked me eagerly, 'Where's the cabin-table?' and to hear such a question was a frightful shock. I had just been blown up, you understand, and vibrated with that experience,—I wasn't quite sure whether I was alive. Mahon began to stamp with both feet and yelled at him, 'Good God! Don't you see the deck's blown out of her?' I found my voice, and stammered out as if conscious of some gross neglect of duty, 'I don't know where the cabin-table is.' It was like an absurd dream.

"Do you know what he wanted next? Well, he wanted to trim the yards. Very placidly, and as if lost in thought, he insisted on having the foreyard squared. 'I don't know if there's anybody alive,' said Mahon, almost tearfully. 'Surely,' he said gently, 'there will be enough left to square the foreyard.'

"The old chap, it seems, was in his own berth, winding up the chronometers, when the shock sent him spinning. Immediately it occurred to him—as he said afterwards—that the ship had struck something, and he ran out into the cabin. There, he saw, the cabin-table had vanished somewhere. The deck being blown up, it had fallen down into the lazarette of course. Where we had our breakfast that morning he saw only a great hole in the floor. This appeared to him so awfully mysterious, and impressed him so immensely, that what he saw and heard after he got on deck were mere trifles in comparison. And, mark, he noticed directly the wheel deserted and his barque off her course—and his only thought was to get that miserable, stripped, undecked, smouldering shell of a ship back again with her head pointing at her port of destination. Bangkok! That's what he was after. I tell you this quiet, bowed, bandy-legged, almost deformed little man was immense in the singleness of his idea and in his placid ignorance of our agitation. He motioned us forward with a commanding gesture, and went to take the wheel himself.

"Yes, that was the first thing we did—trim the yards of that wreck! No one was killed, or even disabled, but everyone was more or less hurt. You should have seen them! Some were in rags, with black faces, like coal-heavers, like sweeps, and had bullet heads that seemed closely cropped, but were in fact singed to the skin. Others, of the watch below, awakened by being shot out from their collapsing bunks, shivered incessantly, and kept on groaning even as we went about our work. But they all worked. That crew of Liverpool hard cases had in them the right stuff. It's my experience they always have. It is the sea that gives it—the vastness, the loneliness surrounding their dark stolid souls. Ah! Well! We stumbled, we crept, we fell, we barked our shins on the wreckage, we hauled. The masts stood, but we did not know how much they might be charred down below. It was nearly calm, but a long swell ran from the west and made her roll. They might go at any moment. We looked at them with apprehension. One could not foresee which way they would fall.

"Then we retreated aft and looked about us. The deck was a tangle of planks on edge, of planks

on end, of splinters, of ruined woodwork. The
masts rose from that chaos like big trees above a
matted undergrowth. The interstices of that mass of
wreckage were full of something whitish, sluggish,
stirring—of something that was like a greasy fog.
The smoke of the invisible fire was coming up again,
was trailing, like a poisonous thick mist in some
valley choked with dead wood. Already lazy wisps
were beginning to curl upwards amongst the mass
of splinters. Here and there a piece of timber, stuck
upright, resembled a post. Half of a fife-rail had
been shot through the foresail, and the sky made a
patch of glorious blue in the ignobly soiled canvas. A
portion of several boards holding together had fallen
across the rail, and one end protruded overboard, like
a gangway leading upon nothing, like a gangway
leading over the deep sea, leading to death—as if
inviting us to walk the plank at once and be done
with our ridiculous troubles. And still the air, the
sky—a ghost, something invisible was hailing the
ship.

"Someone had the sense to look over, and there was the helmsman, who had impulsively jumped overboard, anxious to come back. He yelled and swam lustily like a merman, keeping up with the ship. We threw him a rope, and presently he stood amongst us streaming with water and very crestfallen. The captain had surrendered the wheel, and apart, elbow on rail and chin in hand, gazed at the sea wistfully. We asked ourselves, what next? I thought, Now, this is something like. This is great. I wonder what will happen. O youth!

"Suddenly Mahon sighted a steamer far astern. Captain Beard said, 'We may do something with her yet.' We hoisted two flags, which said in the international language of the sea, 'On fire. Want immediate assistance.' The steamer grew bigger rapidly, and by-and-by spoke with two flags on her foremast, 'I am coming to your assistance.'

"In half an hour she was abreast, to windward, within hail, and rolling slightly, with her engines stopped. We lost our composure, and yelled all together with excitement, 'We've been blown up.' A man in a white helmet, on the bridge, cried, 'Yes! All right! All right!' and he nodded his head, and smiled, and made soothing motions with his hand as though at a lot of frightened children. One of the boats dropped in the water, and walked towards us upon the sea with her long oars. Four Calashes pulled a swinging stroke. This was my first sight of Malay seamen. I've known them since, but what struck me then was their unconcern: they came alongside, and even the bowman standing up and holding to our main-chains with the boat-hook did not deign to lift his head for a glance. I thought people who had been blown up deserved more attention.

"A little man, dry like a chip and agile like a monkey, clambered up. It was the mate of the steamer. He gave one look, and cried, 'O boys—you had better quit.'

"We were silent. He talked apart with the captain for a time,—seemed to argue with him. Then they went away together to the steamer.

"When our skipper came back we learned that the steamer was the Sommerville, Captain Nash, from West Australia to Singapore via Batavia with mails, and that the agreement was she should tow us to Anjer or Batavia, if possible, where we could extinguish the fire by scuttling, and then proceed on our voyage—to Bangkok! The old man seemed excited. 'We will do it yet,' he said to Mahon, fiercely. He shook his fist at the sky. Nobody else said a word.

"At noon the steamer began to tow. She went ahead slim and high, and what was left of the Judea followed at the end of seventy fathom of tow-rope,—followed her swiftly like a cloud of smoke with mastheads protruding above. We went aloft to furl the sails. We coughed on the yards, and were careful about the bunts. Do you see the lot of us there, putting a neat furl on the sails of that ship doomed to arrive nowhere? There was not a man who didn't think that at any moment the masts would topple over. From aloft we could not see the ship for smoke, and they worked carefully, passing the gaskets with even turns. 'Harbour furl—aloft there!' cried Mahon from below.

"You understand this? I don't think one of those chaps expected to get down in the usual way. When we did I heard them saying to each other, 'Well, I thought we would come down overboard, in a lump—sticks and all—blame me if I didn't.' 'That's what I was thinking to myself,' would answer wearily another battered and bandaged scarecrow. And, mind, these were men without the drilled-in habit of obedience. To an onlooker they would be a lot of profane scallywags without a redeeming point. What made them do it—what made them obey me when I, thinking consciously how fine it was, made them drop the bunt of the foresail twice to try and do it better? What? They had no professional reputation—no examples, no praise. It wasn't a sense of duty; they all knew well enough how to shirk, and laze, and dodge—when they had a mind to it—and mostly they had. Was it the two pounds ten a month that sent them there? They didn't think their pay half good enough. No, it was something in them, something inborn and subtle and everlasting. I don't say positively that the crew of a French or German merchantman wouldn't have done it, but I doubt whether it would have been done in the same way. There was a completeness in it, something solid like a principle, and masterful like an instinct— a disclosure of something secret—of that hidden something, that gift, of good or evil that makes racial difference, that shapes the fate of nations.

"It was that night at ten that, for the first time since we had been fighting it, we saw the fire. The speed of the towing had fanned the smoldering destruction. A blue gleam appeared forward, shining below the wreck of the deck. It wavered in patches, it seemed to stir and creep like the light of a glowworm. I saw it first, and told Mahon. 'Then the game's up,' he said. 'We had better stop this towing, or she will burst out suddenly fore and aft before we can clear out.' We set up a yell; rang bells to attract their attention; they towed on. At last Mahon and I had to crawl forward and cut the rope with an ax. There was no time to cast off the lashings. Red tongues could be seen licking the wilderness of splinters under our feet as we made our way back to the poop.

"Of course they very soon found out in the steamer that the rope was gone. She gave a loud blast of her whistle, her lights were seen sweeping in a wide circle, she came up ranging close alongside, and stopped. We were all in a tight group on the poop looking at her. Every man had saved a little bundle or a bag. Suddenly a conical flame with a twisted top shot up forward and threw upon the black sea a circle of light, with the two vessels side by side and heaving gently in its center. Captain Beard had been sitting on the gratings still and mute for hours, but now he rose slowly and advanced in front of us, to the mizzen-shrouds. Captain Nash hailed, 'Come along! Look sharp. I have mail-bags on board. I will take you and your boats to Singapore.'

"'Thank you! No!' said our skipper. 'We must see the last of the ship.'

"'I can't stand by any longer,' shouted the other. 'Mails—you know.'

"'Ay! ay! We are all right.'

"'Very well! I'll report you in Singapore.... Good-bye!'

"He waved his hand. Our men dropped their bundles quietly. The steamer moved ahead, and passing out of the circle of light, vanished at once from our sight, dazzled by the fire which burned fiercely. And then I knew that I would see the East first as commander of a small boat. I thought it fine; and the fidelity to the old ship was fine. We should see the last of her. Oh the glamour of youth! Oh the fire of it, more dazzling than the flames of the burning ship, throwing a magic light on the wide earth, leaping audaciously to the sky, presently to be quenched by time, more cruel, more pitiless, more bitter than the sea—and like the flames of the burning ship surrounded by an impenetrable night.

"The old man warned us in his gentle and inflexible way that it was part of our duty to save for the under-writers as much as we could of the ship's gear. According we went to work aft, while she blazed forward to give us plenty of light. We lugged out a lot of rubbish. What didn't we save? An old barometer fixed with an absurd quantity of screws nearly cost me my life: a sudden rush of smoke came upon me, and I just got away in time. There were various stores, bolts of canvas, coils of rope; the poop looked like a marine bazaar, and the boats were lumbered to the gunwales. One would have thought the old man wanted to take as much as he could of his first command with him. He was very very quiet, but off his balance evidently. Would you believe it? He wanted to take a length of old stream-cable and a kedge-anchor with him in the long-boat. We said, 'Ay, ay, sir,' deferentially, and on the quiet let the thing slip overboard. The heavy medicine-chest went that way, two bags of green coffee, tins of paint—fancy, paint!—a whole lot of things. Then I was ordered with two hands into the boats to make a stowage and get them ready against the time it would be proper for us to leave the ship.

"We put everything straight, stepped the long-boat's mast for our skipper, who was in charge of her, and I was not sorry to sit down for a moment. My face felt raw, every limb ached as if broken, I was aware of all my ribs, and would have sworn to a twist in the back-bone. The boats, fast astern, lay in a deep shadow, and all around I could see the circle of the sea lighted by the fire. A gigantic flame arose forward straight and clear. It flared there, with noises like the whir of wings, with rumbles as of thunder. There were cracks, detonations, and from the cone of flame the sparks flew upwards, as man is born to trouble, to leaky ships, and to ships that burn.

"What bothered me was that the ship, lying broadside to the swell and to such wind as there was—a mere breath—the boats would not keep astern where they were safe, but persisted, in a pig-headed way boats have, in getting under the counter and then swinging alongside. They were knocking about dangerously and coming near the flame, while the ship rolled on them, and, of course, there was always the danger of the masts going over the side at any moment. I and my two boat-keepers kept them off as best we could with oars and boat-hooks; but to be constantly at it became exasperating, since there was no reason why we should not leave at once. We could not see those on board, nor could we imagine what caused the delay. The boat-keepers were swearing feebly, and I had not only my share of the work, but also had to keep at it two men who showed a constant inclination to lay themselves down and let things slide.

"At last I hailed, 'On deck there,' and someone looked over. 'We're ready here,' I said. The head disappeared, and very soon popped up again. 'The captain says, All right, sir, and to keep the boats well clear of the ship.'

"Half an hour passed. Suddenly there was a frightful racket, rattle, clanking of chain, hiss of water, and millions of sparks flew up into the shivering column of smoke that stood leaning slightly above the ship. The cat-heads had burned away, and the two red-hot anchors had gone to the bottom, tearing out after them two hundred fathom of red-hot chain. The ship trembled, the mass of flame swayed as if ready to collapse, and the fore top-gallant-mast fell. It darted down like an arrow of fire, shot under, and instantly leaping up within an oar's-length of the boats, floated quietly, very black on the luminous sea. I hailed the deck again. After some time a man in an unexpectedly cheerful but also muffled tone, as though he had been trying to speak with his mouth shut, informed me, 'Coming directly, sir,' and vanished. For a long time I heard nothing but the whir and roar of the fire. There were also whistling sounds. The boats jumped, tugged at the painters, ran at each other playfully, knocked their sides together, or, do what we would, swung in a bunch against the ship's side. I couldn't stand it any longer, and swarming up a rope, clambered aboard over the stern.

"It was as bright as day. Coming up like this, the sheet of fire facing me was a terrifying sight, and the heat seemed hardly bearable at first. On a settee cushion dragged out of the cabin, Captain Beard, with his legs drawn up and one arm under his head, slept with the light playing on him. Do you know what the rest were busy about? They were sitting on deck right aft, round an open case, eating bread and cheese and drinking bottled stout.

"On the background of flames twisting in fierce tongues above their heads they seemed at home like salamanders, and looked like a band of desperate pirates. The fire sparkled in the whites of their eyes, gleamed on patches of white skin seen through the torn shirts. Each had the marks as of a battle about him—bandaged heads, tied-up arms, a strip of dirty rag round a knee—and each man had a bottle between his legs and a chunk of cheese in his hand. Mahon got up. With his handsome and disreputable head, his hooked profile, his long white beard, and with an uncorked bottle in his hand, he resembled one of those reckless sea-robbers of old making merry amidst violence and disaster. 'The last meal on board,' he explained solemnly. 'We had nothing to eat all day, and it was no use leaving all this.' He flourished the bottle and indicated the sleeping skipper. 'He said he couldn't swallow anything, so I got him to lie down,' he went on; and as I stared, 'I don't know whether you are aware, young fellow, the man had no sleep to speak of for days—and there will be dam' little sleep in the boats.' 'There will be no boats by-and-by if you fool about much longer,' I said, indignantly. I walked up to the skipper and shook him by the shoulder. At last he opened his eyes, but did not move. 'Time to leave her, sir,' I said, quietly.

"He got up painfully, looked at the flames, at the sea sparkling round the ship, and black, black as ink farther away; he looked at the stars shining dim through a thin veil of smoke in a sky black, black as Erebus.

"'Youngest first,' he said.

"And the ordinary seaman, wiping his mouth with the back of his hand, got up, clambered over the taffrail, and vanished. Others followed. One, on the point of going over, stopped short to drain his bottle, and with a great swing of his arm flung it at the fire. 'Take this!' he cried.

"The skipper lingered disconsolately, and we left him to commune alone for a while with his first command. Then I went up again and brought him away at last. It was time. The ironwork on the poop was hot to the touch.

"Then the painter of the long-boat was cut, and the three boats, tied together, drifted clear of the ship. It was just sixteen hours after the explosion when we abandoned her. Mahon had charge of the second boat, and I had the smallest—the 14-foot thing. The long-boat would have taken the lot of us; but the skipper said we must save as much property as we could—for the under-writers—and so I got my first command. I had two men with me, a bag of biscuits, a few tins of meat, and a breaker of water. I was ordered to keep close to the long-boat, that in case of bad weather we might be taken into her.

"And do you know what I thought? I thought I would part company as soon as I could. I wanted to have my first command all to myself. I wasn't going to sail in a squadron if there were a chance for independent cruising. I would make land by myself. I would beat the other boats. Youth! All youth! The silly, charming, beautiful youth.

"But we did not make a start at once. We must see the last of the ship. And so the boats drifted about that night, heaving and setting on the swell. The men dozed, waked, sighed, groaned. I looked at the burning ship.

"Between the darkness of earth and heaven she was burning fiercely upon a disc of purple sea shot by the blood-red play of gleams; upon a disc of water glittering and sinister. A high, clear flame, an immense and lonely flame, ascended from the ocean, and from its summit the black smoke poured continuously at the sky. She burned furiously, mournful and imposing like a funeral pile kindled in the night, surrounded by the sea, watched over by the stars. A magnificent death had come like a grace, like a gift, like a reward to that old ship at the end of her laborious days. The surrender of her weary ghost to the keeping of stars and sea was stirring like the sight of a glorious triumph. The masts fell just before daybreak, and for a moment there was a burst and turmoil of sparks that seemed to fill with flying fire the night patient and watchful, the vast night lying silent upon the sea. At daylight she was only a charred shell, floating still under a cloud of smoke and bearing a glowing mass of coal within.

"Then the oars were got out, and the boats forming in a line moved round her remains as if in procession—the long-boat leading. As we pulled across her stern a slim dart of fire shot out viciously at us, and suddenly she went down, head first, in a great hiss of steam. The unconsumed stern was the last to sink; but the paint had gone, had cracked, had peeled off, and there were no letters, there was no word, no stubborn device that was like her soul, to flash at the rising sun her creed and her name.

"We made our way north. A breeze sprang up, and about noon all the boats came together for the last time. I had no mast or sail in mine, but I made a mast out of a spare oar and hoisted a boat-awning for a sail, with a boat-hook for a yard. She was certainly over-masted, but I had the satisfaction of knowing that with the wind aft I could beat the other two. I had to wait for them. Then we all had a look at the captain's chart, and, after a sociable meal of hard bread and water, got our last instructions. These were simple: steer north, and keep together as much as possible. 'Be careful with that jury rig, Marlow,' said the captain; and Mahon, as I sailed proudly past his boat, wrinkled his curved nose and hailed, 'You will sail that ship of yours under water, if you don't look out, young fellow.' He was a malicious old man— and may the deep sea where he sleeps now rock him gently, rock him tenderly to the end of time!

"Before sunset a thick rain-squall passed over the two boats, which were far astern, and that was the last I saw of them for a time. Next day I sat steering my cockle-shell—my first command—with nothing but water and sky around me. I did sight in the afternoon the upper sails of a ship far away, but said nothing, and my men did not notice her. You see I was afraid she might be homeward bound, and I had no mind to turn back from the portals of the East. I was steering for Java—another blessed name—like Bangkok, you know. I steered many days.

"I need not tell you what it is to be knocking about in an open boat. I remember nights and days of calm when we pulled, we pulled, and the boat seemed to stand still, as if bewitched within the circle of the sea horizon. I remember the heat, the deluge of rain-squalls that kept us baling for dear life (but filled our water-cask), and I remember sixteen hours on end with a mouth dry as a cinder and a steering-oar over the stern to keep my first command head on to a breaking sea. I did not know how good a man I was till then. I remember the drawn faces, the dejected figures of my two men, and I remember my youth and the feeling that will never come back any more—the feeling that I could last for ever, outlast the sea, the earth, and all men; the deceitful feeling that lures us on to joys, to perils, to love, to vain effort—to death; the triumphant conviction of strength, the heat of life in the handful of dust, the glow in the heart that with every year grows dim, grows cold, grows small, and expires—and expires, too soon—before life itself.

"And this is how I see the East. I have seen its secret places and have looked into its very soul; but now I see it always from a small boat, a high outline of mountains, blue and afar in the morning; like faint mist at noon; a jagged wall of purple at sunset. I have the feel of the oar in my hand, the vision of a scorching blue sea in my eyes. And I see a bay, a wide bay, smooth as glass and polished like ice, shimmering in the dark. A red light burns far off upon the gloom of the land, and the night is soft and warm. We drag at the oars with aching arms, and suddenly a puff of wind, a puff faint and tepid and laden with strange odors of blossoms, of aromatic wood, comes out of the still night—the first sigh of the East on my face. That I can never forget. It was impalpable and enslaving, like a charm, like a whispered promise of mysterious delight.

"We had been pulling this finishing spell for eleven hours. Two pulled, and he whose turn it was to rest sat at the tiller. We had made out the red light in that bay and steered for it, guessing it must mark some small coasting port. We passed two vessels, outlandish and high-sterned, sleeping at anchor, and, approaching the light, now very dim, ran the boat's nose against the end of a jutting wharf. We were blind with fatigue. My men dropped the oars and fell off the thwarts as if dead. I made fast to a pile. A current rippled softly. The scented obscurity of the shore was grouped into vast masses, a density of colossal clumps of vegetation, probably—mute and fantastic shapes. And at their foot the semicircle of a beach gleamed faintly, like an illusion. There was not a light, not a stir, not a sound. The mysterious East faced me, perfumed like a flower, silent like death, dark like a grave.

"And I sat weary beyond expression, exulting like a conqueror, sleepless and entranced as if before a profound, a fateful enigma.

"A splashing of oars, a measured dip reverberating on the level of water, intensified by the silence of the shore into loud claps, made me jump up. A boat, a European boat, was coming in. I invoked the name of the dead; I hailed: Judea ahoy! A thin shout answered.

"It was the captain. I had beaten the flagship by three hours, and I was glad to hear the old man's voice, tremulous and tired. 'Is it you, Marlow?' 'Mind the end of that jetty, sir,' I cried.

"He approached cautiously, and brought up with the deep-sea lead-line which we had saved—for the under-writers. I eased my painter and fell alongside.

He sat, a broken figure at the stern, wet with dew, his hands clasped in his lap. His men were asleep already. 'I had a terrible time of it,' he murmured. 'Mahon is behind—not very far.' We conversed in whispers, in low whispers, as if afraid to wake up the land. Guns, thunder, earthquakes would not have awakened the men just then.

"Looking around as we talked, I saw away at sea a bright light travelling in the night. 'There's a steamer passing the bay,' I said. She was not passing, she was entering, and she even came close and anchored. 'I wish,' said the old man, 'you would find out whether she is English. Perhaps they could give us a passage somewhere.' He seemed nervously anxious. So by dint of punching and kicking I started one of my men into a state of somnambulism, and giving him an oar, took another and pulled towards the lights of the steamer.

"There was a murmur of voices in her, metallic hollow clangs of the engine-room, footsteps on the deck. Her ports shone, round like dilated eyes.

Shapes moved about, and there was a shadowy man high up on the bridge. He heard my oars.

"And then, before I could open my lips, the East spoke to me, but it was in a Western voice. A torrent of words was poured into the enigmatical, the fateful silence; outlandish, angry words, mixed with words and even whole sentences of good English, less strange but even more surprising. The voice swore and cursed violently; it riddled the solemn peace of the bay by a volley of abuse. It began by calling me Pig, and from that went crescendo into unmentionable adjectives—in English. The man up there raged aloud in two languages, and with a sincerity in his fury that almost convinced me I had, in some way, sinned against the harmony of the universe. I could hardly see him, but began to think he would work himself into a fit.

"Suddenly he ceased, and I could hear him snorting and blowing like a porpoise. I said—

"'What steamer is this, pray?'

"'Eh? What's this? And who are you?'

"'Castaway crew of an English barque burnt at sea. We came here to-night. I am the second mate. The captain is in the long-boat, and wishes to know if you would give us a passage somewhere.'

"'Oh, my goodness! I say... This is the Celestial from Singapore on her return trip. I'll arrange with your captain in the morning... and... I say... did you hear me just now?'

"'I should think the whole bay heard you.'

"'I thought you were a shore-boat. Now, look here—this infernal lazy scoundrel of a caretaker has gone to sleep again—curse him. The light is out, and I nearly ran foul of the end of this damned jetty. This is the third time he plays me this trick. Now, I ask you, can anybody stand this kind of thing? It's enough to drive a man out of his mind. I'll report him.... I'll get the Assistant Resident to give him the sack, by... See—there's no light. It's out, isn't it? I take you to witness the light's out. There should be a light, you know. A red light on the—'

"'There was a light,' I said, mildly.

"'But it's out, man! What's the use of talking like this? You can see for yourself it's out—don't you? If you had to take a valuable steamer along this God-forsaken coast you would want a light too. I'll kick him from end to end of his miserable wharf. You'll see if I don't. I will—'

"'So I may tell my captain you'll take us?' I broke in.

"'Yes, I'll take you. Good night,' he said, brusquely.

"I pulled back, made fast again to the jetty, and then went to sleep at last. I had faced the silence of the East. I had heard some of its languages. But when I opened my eyes again the silence was as complete as though it had never been broken. I was lying in a flood of light, and the sky had never looked so far, so high, before. I opened my eyes and lay without moving.

"And then I saw the men of the East—they were looking at me. The whole length of the jetty was full of people. I saw brown, bronze, yellow faces, the black eyes, the glitter, the colour of an Eastern crowd. And all these beings stared without a murmur, without a sigh, without a movement. They stared down at the boats, at the sleeping men who at night had come to them from the sea. Nothing moved. The fronds of palms stood still against the sky. Not a branch stirred along the shore, and the brown roofs of hidden houses peeped through the green foliage, through the big leaves that hung shining and still like leaves forged of heavy metal. This was the East of the ancient navigators, so old, so mysterious, resplendent and somber, living and unchanged, full of danger and promise. And these were the men. I sat up suddenly. A wave of movement passed through the crowd from end to end, passed along the heads, swayed the bodies, ran along the jetty like a ripple on the water, like a breath of wind on a field—and all was still again. I see it now—the wide sweep of the bay, the glittering sands, the wealth of green infinite and varied, the sea blue like the sea of a dream, the crowd of attentive faces, the blaze of vivid colour—the water reflecting it all, the curve of the shore, the jetty, the high-sterned outlandish craft floating still, and the three boats with tired men from the West sleeping unconscious of the land and the people and of the violence of sunshine. They slept thrown across the thwarts, curled on bottom-boards, in the careless attitudes of death. The head of the old skipper, leaning back in the stern of the long-boat, had fallen on his breast, and he looked as though he would never wake. Farther out old Mahon's face was upturned to the sky, with the long white beard spread out on his breast, as though he had been shot where he sat at the tiller; and a man, all in a heap in the bows of the boat, slept with both arms embracing the stem-head and with his cheek laid on the gunwale. The East looked at them without a sound.

"I have known its fascination since: I have seen the mysterious shores, the still water, the lands of brown nations, where a stealthy Nemesis lies in wait, pursues, overtakes so many of the conquering race, who are proud of their wisdom, of their knowledge, of their strength. But for me all the East is contained in that vision of my youth. It is all in that moment when I opened my young eyes on it. I came upon it from a tussle with the sea—and I was young—and I saw it looking at me. And this is all that is left of it! Only a moment; a moment of strength, of romance, of glamour—of youth! ... A flick of sunshine upon a strange shore, the time to remember, the time for a sigh, and—good-bye!—Night—Good-bye...!"

He drank.

"Ah! The good old time—the good old time. Youth and the sea. Glamour and the sea! The good, strong sea, the salt, bitter sea, that could whisper to you and roar at you and knock your breath out of you."

He drank again.

"By all that's wonderful, it is the sea, I believe, the sea itself—or is it youth alone? Who can tell? But you here—you all had something out of life: money, love—whatever one gets on shore—and, tell me, wasn't that the best time, that time when we were young at sea; young and had nothing, on the sea that gives nothing, except hard knocks—and sometimes a chance to feel your strength—that only—what you all regret?"

And we all nodded at him: the man of finance, the man of accounts, the man of law, we all nodded at him over the polished table that like a still sheet of brown water reflected our faces, lined, wrinkled; our faces marked by toil, by deceptions, by success, by love; our weary eyes looking still, looking always, looking anxiously for something out of life, that while it is expected is already gone—has passed unseen, in a sigh, in a flash—together with the youth, with the strength, with the romance of illusions.

附:

作者简介

梁遇春

Joseph Conrad（1857—1924），他的名字正式写起来是 Josef Teodor Konrad Korzeniowski。他的父亲是波兰的地主，非常爱国，总想使波兰能够恢复独立的地位。1863 年革命失败，被流徙到 Vologda 去。他的母亲也自愿到这荒凉的地方去做苦工，跟她丈夫做伴，可是身体太弱，不久就过世了。他父亲后来虽然放回来，可惜没有多久也死了。于是我们这位二十年沧海寄身的文豪十二岁时就成为一个孤儿。

他幼年时候对于海就有极强的趣味，成人后决心当个舟子，不管戚友种种劝诱，终于扬帆跟孤舟去相依为命。他的父亲曾将莎士比亚、嚣俄（雨果，法国作家——编辑注）译成荷文，他很早就博览文学作品，深有文学情调。海上无事时随便写下一本长篇小说，有时间断，有时接续下去，一共写了五年，脱稿后还搁置了许久。后来偶然碰到一位搭客，读他的稿子，劝他出版，这算做他文学生涯的开始，这位上帝派来的搭客就是现在英国最伟大的小说家 John Galsworthy。

他的著作都是以海洋做题材，但是他不像普通海洋作家那样只会肤浅地描写海上的风浪；他是能抓到海上的一种情调，写出满纸的波涛，使人们有一个整个的神秘感觉。他对于船仿佛看做是一个人，他书里的每只船都有特别的性格，简直跟别个小说家书里的英雄一样。然而，他自己最注重的却是船里面个个海员性格的刻画。他的人物不是代表那一类人的，每人有他绝对显明的个性，你念过后永不会忘却，但是写得一点不勉强，一点不夸张，这真是像从作者的灵魂开出的朵朵鲜花。这几个妙处凑起来使他的小说愈读，回甘的意味愈永。

他的著作有二十余册，最有名的是《Lord Jim》《The Nigger of the "Narcissus"》《Nostromo》等长篇小说，《Youth》《Typhon》《The Heart of Darkness》等短篇小说，还有几本散文《A Personal

Record》《The Mirror of the Sea》《Notes on Life and Letters》，里面尤以《海镜》极能道出海的无限神秘。

这篇是他最有名的短篇小说，里面的事实却是真的，那是他 1881 年第一次到东方去的冒险故事。亲身经历过的事情因为对于自己太有趣味了，写出来常常平凡得可怜。自己觉得有意思，就以为别人一定也会喜欢，这是许多自传小说家的毛病。一篇自述的东西能够写得这么好像完全出于幻想的，玲珑得似非人世间的事实，从这一点也可以看出这位老舟子的艺术手腕同成就了。

谈梁遇春

冯　至

　　近几年来，常有研究中国现代散文的同志约我写篇文章谈谈梁遇春。我想，比较更深地了解梁遇春的朋友和同学多已去世，我和梁遇春交往虽然不久，在 1930 年从晚春到初秋不过五六个月，却也共同度过些只有年轻人才能享有的愉快的时日，我对于这个要求有义不容辞之感。但是我那时不写日记，信件也不知保存，随着岁月的流逝，当年亲切的会晤已变得模糊不清，饶有风趣的交谈也只剩下东鳞西爪。在那"忘形到尔汝"的时刻，我怎么会想到半个多世纪后要搜索枯肠，追思往事，写这样的回忆呢？

　　这是我答应写这篇文章时思想里直接的反应。可是经过一番考虑，想到我这不幸早年逝世的朋友，想到他的为人、他的风姿、他的文采，我不应用"搜索枯肠"来对付。我应该认真再读一遍他留给我们的两本散文集《春醪集》和《泪与笑》，以无限的怀念之情实事求是地把模糊不清的事想得清楚一些，给残存的片言只语寻得一些线索，当然，更重要的还是根据他的散文谈一谈这个年轻的思考者在他那个时代想了些什么。

这是文学史里的一种现象，有少数华年早丧的诗人，像是稀有的彗星忽然出现在天边，放射异样的光芒，不久便消逝。他们仿佛预感自己将不久于人世，迫不及待地要为人类做出一点贡献，往往当众多"大器晚成"享有高龄的作家不慌不忙地或者尚未开始写作时，他们则以惊人的才力，呕心沥血，谱写下瑰丽的诗篇。他们的思想格外活跃，感触格外锐敏，经历虽然不多，生活却显得格外灿烂，在短暂的时期内真可以说是春花怒放。我的这个看法，难免招来唯心或宿命之讥，我自己也不认为是正确的，但例如中国的李贺、英国的济慈、德国的诺瓦利斯等人，确实是这样，他们的创作时期极为短促，论成绩则抵得住或者超过有些著名诗人几十年的努力成果。梁遇春的成就虽不能与列举的那几位短命诗人相比，但他短暂的一生中工作的勤奋却与他们很相似。他从1926年冬开始发表散文，到1932年夏他27岁逝世不满六年的时间内，写了36篇闪耀着智慧光辉、具有独特风格的散文。他拼命地阅读古今中外的书籍，翻译外国文学作品20余种，其中英汉对照的《英国诗歌选》，有在三四十年代攻读过英国文学的大学生，在他们已将进入老年的今天，还乐于称道这本书，说从中获益匪浅。梁遇春没有创作过诗，但他有诗人的气质，他的散文洋溢着浓郁的诗情。

梁遇春在他第一本散文集《春醪集》第一篇题名《讲演》的散文里说："近来我很爱胡思乱想，但是越想越不明白一切事情的道理。"紧接着他说，他同意"作《平等阁笔记》的主笔所谓世界中不只'无奇不有'，实在是'无有不奇'"。这段话，他写的时候不过22岁，却可以作为他此后六年所写的散文共同的题词。"胡思乱想"是自谦之词，实际上说明他开动脑筋，勤于思考，事事都要问个是什么、为什么。"不明白一切事情的道理"，才能促使人追根究底，把事情弄明白些。在弄明白的过程中，便会发现世界上的事不仅"无奇不有",而且"无有不奇"。这里所说的"奇",我看有双重意义:一是"新奇"的奇,是从平凡的生活中看出"新";一是"奇怪"的奇,是从社会上不合理而又习以为常的事物中看到"怪"。至于思想怠惰、遇事随声附和、自以为一切都明白了的人们不可能发现什么"新",更不会感觉到"怪"。梁遇春则是从"胡思乱想"开始,写他字里行间既新奇又奇怪的散文。但他的散文委婉自如,并不标新立异,故作惊人之笔。

梁遇春在他的散文里一再说,矛盾是宇宙的根本原理,自然界和人世间无穷无尽的矛盾是"数千年来贤哲所追求的宇宙的本质"。他还引用萧伯纳的话:"天下充满了矛盾的事情,只是我们没有去思考,所以看不见了。"我们无须说,梁遇春懂得多少辩证法,可是他确实从书本上、从对于宇宙和人生的探索和观察中,领悟到一切事物内存在着矛盾,而且他很欣赏那些矛盾。他热爱人类。他1930年写的《救火夫》是他散文中最有积极意义的名篇。他看见某处失火,救火的人们争先恐后奔赴火场,把生死置之度外,他们多半素不相识，但在救火时都成为互助的同志，他们也不问失火的那家主人是好人或是坏蛋，那时他们去救的好像不是某个个人，而是"人类"。他热情颂扬救火的人们，谴责隔岸看火的旁观者。同时他认为，如今全世界，至少在中国，到处都着了火，如果见火不救，就等于对人类失职。他说他三年来的"宏愿"是想当个救火夫。但他的"宏愿"并没有实现，他直到逝世只不过是一个对人类抱有悲悯之情的旁观者。他自身内在就存在着一个这样的矛盾。

他赞美光明。他认为只有深知黑暗的人才会热烈地赞美光明，同样，想知道黑暗的人最少总得有光明的心地。他列举某些著名的作家和作品，说明在黑暗中受过苦难和考验的人最能迫切地向往光明，反过来说，若是谁的心里没有光明，也不能真正描写黑暗，像一度流行的黑幕小说，只能污染读者的心灵。

他说，希望是一服包医百病的良方。希望的来源是烦恼，因为烦恼使人不得不有希望；希望的去处应该是圆满和成功。可是圆满的地位等于死刑的宣告，成功的代价是使人感觉迟钝，不再前进。他说他喜欢读屠格涅夫的小说，由于"屠格涅夫所深恶的人是那班成功的人"，他从中推论出"值得我们可怜的绝不是一败涂地的，却是事事马到功成的所谓幸运人们"。

关于道德，他在《查理斯·兰姆评传》中说，兰姆的"道德观念却非常重。他用非常诚恳态度采取道德观念，什么事情一定要寻根到底赤裸裸地来审察，绝不容有丝毫伪君子成分在他心中。也是因为他对道德态度是忠实，所以他又常主张我们有时应当取一种无道德态度，把道德观念撇开一边不管，自由地来品评艺术和生活"。这里说的是兰姆，其实也是梁遇春自己的意见。他最憎恶伪君子，因为"伪君子们对道德没有真情感，只有一副空架子，记着几句口头禅，无处不说他们的套语，一时不肯放松将道德存起来，这是等于做贼心虚，更用心保持他好人的外表……只有自己问心无愧的人才敢有时放了道德的严肃面孔，同大家痛快地毫无拘管地说笑"。梁遇春的散文，就给人以一种印象，作者毫无拘束地面对读者说自己心里的真话。

以上仅就梁遇春对于人类和道德的态度，对

于光明和黑暗、希望与成功的看法这几点，说明他为什么认为矛盾是宇宙的本质，为什么他看世界上的事物有的是新奇，有的是奇怪。这是他散文的根本精神。废名在他给《泪与笑》写的序里说："他的文思如星珠串天，处处闪眼，然而没有一个线索，稍纵即逝。"这句话常被梁遇春散文的评论者援引，认为说得中肯，我则认为这句话只形了梁遇春散文的风格，至于散文中的思想，如前所述，还是有线索可寻的。

他博览群书，他受影响较多的，大体看来有下边的三个方面：他从英国的散文学习到如何观察人生，从中国的诗尤其是从宋人的诗词学习到如何吟味人生，从俄罗斯的小说学习到如何挖掘人生。这当然不能包括他读到的所有书籍。不管这三个范畴以内或以外，许多书中的隽语警句他在文章里经常引用，它们有的与他原来的思想相契合，有的像一把钥匙打开了他的思路，但也有时引用过多，给文章添了些不必要的累赘。

他勤于阅读，尊重知识，却又蔑视知识的"贩卖者"。他写过一篇《论知识贩卖所的伙计》，对于教师们尤其是大学教授很不恭敬。文章一开始就引用了威廉·詹姆士一句尖锐刺耳的话："每门学问的天生仇敌是那门的教授。"这话说得相当偏激，但在文学这一门里，的确有些生趣盎然的作品，经大学教授一讲，便索然无味，不仅不能引起学生欣赏的兴趣，反而使学生对那些作品发生反感。我听有人对我说过，他后悔很晚才读莎士比亚，其原因就是作学生时听过莎士比亚这门课，使他长时期不想和莎士比亚的作品接近。梁遇春大半有鉴于此，他认为在课堂里听教授讲课，无异于浪费光阴，在课外还去听名人演讲，更是自寻苦恼。他惯于跟教授学者们开玩笑，唱对台戏。约在1924—1925年间北京有些教授学者开展过一次关于人生观的论战，他则在这场论战无结果而散的两年后，写了一篇《人死观》；后来又有些教授学者郑重讨论英语里的Gentleman这个词怎样翻译才准确，他却撰写长文歌颂 Gentleman 对立面的人物——流浪汉，说惠特曼的《草叶集》是流浪汉的圣经。他列举许多富有叛逆精神的流浪汉，以极大的痛苦和快乐，写下激动人心的不朽名著，却被循规蹈矩、思想感情都僵化的教授们在课堂里讲解剖析，岂不是一个很大的笑话！

梁遇春这样蔑视听课，"诋毁"教授，可是他从 1922 年到 1928 年在北京大学上过六年学，从 1928 年到 1932 年在上海和北京的大学里当过四年助教，前前后后，他也算是在他所谓的知识贩卖所里当了十年的"伙计"。他这个伙计是怎么当的，我不清楚。但有一种情况我是清楚的，他在北大英文系的学习成绩是优良的，并且得到个别教授的赞赏。1928 年由于政局的关系，北京大学的工作陷于停顿，北大英文系教授温源宁去上海暨南大学任教，就把刚毕业的梁遇春介绍到暨南大学当助教，1930 年温源宁返回北大，他也跟着回来，管理英文系的图书并兼任助教。由此可见，他这个"伙计"当得还是不错的。

梁遇春于 1922 年暑假考入北京大学预科，比我晚一年。那时北大预科在东华门内北河沿北大第三院上课。我常常看到他。由于他显得年轻聪颖，走路时头部略微向前探，有特殊的风姿，而且往往是独来独往，这都引起我的注意。我不记得什么时候才知道他的姓名，却总没有结识的机会，更不知道他的头脑里蕴蓄着那么多丰富而又新奇的思想。直到 1927 年后，才先后在《语丝》《奔流》等刊物上读到他的散文，并且在 1930 年知道他出版了一本散文集《春醪集》。

1930 年从 5 月到 9 月，我和废名在北平办过一个小型周刊《骆驼草》，里边登载过几篇梁遇春（秋心）的散文，原稿最初是废名拿来的，不久我和他也渐渐熟识了。我身边没有《骆驼草》，无从查考梁遇春的哪些文章是在这刊物上发表的。我只记得他的三篇关于爱情的文章曾引起我的惊讶。这三篇散文的标题是《她走了》《苦笑》《坟》，读后的印象觉得它们既是用散文写的抒情诗，又是用诗的语言写的爱情论。这三篇每篇各自以"她走了""你走了""你走后"为首句，像一组"走了"的三部曲，说尽了爱人走后一片错综复杂的凄苦心情，对于人生有一层又一层深入的体会。第一篇里他说，"命运的手支配着我的手写这篇文字"。第二篇是痛苦的断念。第三篇则是"叫自己不要胡用心力，因为'想你'是罪过，可说是对你犯一种罪。……然而，'不想你'

也是罪过,对于自己的罪过"。在这样的矛盾中只好什么也不想,可是心里又不是空无一物,却是有了一座坟,"小影心头葬"。作者说,"我觉得这一座坟是很美的,因为天下美的东西都是使人们看着心酸的"。这最后一句话涵义很深,在当时一般文艺作品里是读不到的。

这三篇文章是用"秋心"笔名发表的。在我初读原稿以及校对清样时,已经感到惊奇,不久我又知道,他写这三篇文章,他的妻子正住在妇产医院里。妇女分娩,是希望与痛苦并存、生的快乐与死的担心互相消长的时刻,梁遇春独自在家里的灯下写这样的文字,到底是什么意思呢?我更无从得到解答。这里所说的"她"是另一个人呢,还是象征他的妻子,认为孩子一降生,往日的爱情就会变成另一个样子?或者"她"既不是另一个人,也不是象征他的妻子,而是个抽象的人物?后来我在《春醪集》里读到两篇《寄给一个失恋人的信》,收信人的名字也叫"秋心",我才若有所悟,原来那位虚构的收信人如今现身说法了。在那两封信里,写信人畅谈易逝的青春如何值得爱恋,"当初"是如何永远可贵(因为一般失恋者常说"既有今日，何必当初"那类的话），变更是不可抗拒的自然规律。他劝人不要羡慕得意的人们，"人生最可怕的是得意，使人精神废弛一切灰心的事情无过于不散的筵席"。写给"秋心"的两封信和署名"秋心"的三篇散文，二者写作的时间相隔两三年，却可以互相补充，表达了梁遇春的恋爱观。

我对那三篇散文虽然有过疑问，但我和遇春见面时从未问过他是怎么写出来的。后来他的妻子出院了（那时产妇住院的时间比较长些），他这样的文章也从此搁笔了。一天，我到他在北池子租赁的寓所找他，他的妻子已出满月，按照南方的习惯，煮了美味的汤圆招待我，他抱出他新生的女儿给我看，同时他说："在这'曾是年华磨灭地'，听着婴儿的啼声，心里有一种难以形容的又苦又甜的滋味。"

我到他家里只去过一次，他到我的住处次数也不多，但是我们常常会面，我想不起我们都是怎么遇合的，只记得我们的畅谈多半是在公园的茶桌旁。我们谈人生，谈艺术，谈读书的心得，他心胸开阔，正如他说的，"对于知己的朋友老是这么露骨地乱谈着"。那时我们有一个共同的脾气，不喜欢四平八稳、满口道德语言的正人君子，觉得这样的人不容易接近，也不必接近。我曾向他称道张岱的《陶庵梦忆》里的一句话："人无癖不可与交，以其无深情也；人无疵不可与交，以其无真气也。"人无完人，总会有这样那样的缺点，假如有个人给人以印象，一点毛病也没有，那就是遮羞盖耻的伪君子，对人不会以真诚相见，同样，一个人如果事事都不即不离，无所偏好，更谈不上对某件事锲而不舍，这样的人不可能有深厚的感情。遇春同意我的意见，他说："宋朝有个宰相，一生官运亨通，既无深情，也无至性，告老还乡后，倒说了一句真心话：'一辈子逢人就做笑脸，只笑得满脸都是皱纹。'你看，这是多么一副丑相！"他说时没有说出宰相的姓名，我也无从查考这句话的出处了。

我们还欣赏那时不知从哪里听来的一句诗："六朝人物晚唐诗。"在六朝和晚唐极其混乱的时代，能产生那么多超脱成规、鄙夷礼教的人物和一往情深、沁人肺腑的诗篇，是中国历史上特殊的光彩，我们不同意有些人把他们与西方世纪末的颓废派相提并论。

我们上天下地无所不谈，但两个人好像不约而同，也有所不谈。一、不在背后议论共同的朋友和熟人。二、不谈个人的苦恼。梁遇春在《坟》里转述友人沉海的话："诉自己的悲哀，求人们给以同情，是等于叫花子露出胸前的创伤，请过路人施舍。"我不知"沉海"是谁。我记得我也说过这类的话。三、不谈个人的家世。他的家庭情况，我一无所知。只有一次例外，我去德国前，他说他有一个叔父在德国学医，但没有告诉我他叔父在德国的地址。

我在 1930 年 9 月下旬到德国后，我们通信不多，我有时在报刊上读到他新发表的文字。1932 年夏，我在柏林读里尔克晚年的两部诗集《杜伊诺哀歌》和《致奥尔弗斯的十四行诗》，在十四行诗里读到："苦难没有认清，／爱也没有学成，／远远在死乡的事物，／没有揭开了面幕"，我想起遇春的散文《人死观》里有类似的思想。在哀歌的第一首里读到："因为美无异于／我们还能担当的恐怖之开端"，又使我想起，这与《坟》

里的那句"天下美的东西都是使人们看着心酸的"也有些相似。我很想把这些诗写给他,和他讨论,不料一天在国内寄来的报纸上读到梁遇春逝世的消息,这对我是怎么也意想不到的事。为了排解哀思,我到德国东海吕根岛上做了一个星期的旅行,一路上,遇春的言谈面貌总在萦绕着我,我应该用什么来纪念他呢?

　　1937 年,我在上海写了《给秋心》四首诗,在一个文学杂志上发表,1942 年我出版《十四行集》,曾把这四首诗作为杂诗附印在十四行的后边。1949 年《十四行集》重版,我觉得这四首诗对于亡友的怀念表达得很不够,又把它们删去了。过了 30 年,我从中选出两首,编入 1980 年出版的《冯至诗选》里,诗的题目改为《给亡友梁遇春》。我在第一首里说,有些老年人好像跟死断绝了关联,反而在青年身上却潜伏着死的预感。诗的最后两行是:

　　　　你像是一个灿烂的春

　　　　沉在夜里,宁静而黑暗。

第二首大意是，我曾意外地遇见过素不相识的人，我和他们有的在树林里共同走过一段小路，有的在车中谈过一次心，有的在筵席间问过名姓，可是一转眼便各自东西，想再见也难以找到。这首诗是这样收尾的：

你可是也参入他们

生疏的队伍，让我寻找？

可是我不能再找到他了，我把他安排在一个春夜里、一个生疏的队伍里，是幻想着他仍然存在。

40年代初，我在昆明却有一次遇见梁遇春在德国学过医的叔父。抗日战争时期，大批文化教育工作者、自由职业者退入内地。我偶然听说他的叔父在昆明行医，便去拜访他，谈到他侄子的早逝，他不胜惋惜。他身边有一幅遇春的女儿的照片，他拿出来给我看，是一个十岁左右的活泼的女孩。我端详许久，舍不得放下，我当时竟那样神不守舍，连她的名字叫什么都忘了问一问。她如果健在，现在应该是50多岁了，他三岁丧父，但愿父亲在一个婴儿的头脑里还留下一个亲爱的影像。

　　许多青年时的朋友后来都有较大的变化。遇春如不早逝，他一定也会有变化的。从他散文里的迹象看来，他也许后来摒弃了旁观者的态度，实现他那"救火夫"的宏愿，成为革命者。他在大学里工作，勤勤恳恳，最后也许成为一门学问的"天生仇敌"——大学教授；他也许成长为一个优秀的评论家，因为《泪与笑》最后的一篇评论英国传记作家齐尔兹·栗董·斯特拉奇的长文，品评得失，持论透彻精辟，就是放在我们现在有关外国文学的论文中，也毫不逊色；他也许会写出更多优秀的散文，成为中国的兰姆。这些只能由我们虚无缥缈地去推测，永远不会成为事实。刘国平在为《泪与笑》写的序里引用过梁遇春的一句话："青年时候死去，在他人的记忆里永远是年轻的。"这句话一点也不错，遇春在我的记忆里永远是年轻的。

　　最后，我有一句声明。我只是如实地谈一谈我所知道的梁遇春，并不是要宣扬梁遇春那样的思想。我认为，若有人下点功夫，研究一下

"五四"后十几年内各种类型的青年人的思想，对于我们研究现代文学还是有用处的。

1983 年 8 月 27 日